BOOKS

FROM WRITER TO READER

BOOKS

FROM WRITER TO READER

HOWARD GREENFELD

Crown Publishers, Inc., New York

PHOTO CREDITS:
Aldus, 58, 80, 81; Apple Computer, Inc., 114, 183; Compugraphic, 182; Heidelberg Eastern, Inc., 140, 142, 143; Linotype Corporation, 106, 111; Magna, 114; Murray Printing Company, 101; Visual Graphics Corporation, 108.

Published by Crown Publishers, Inc., 225 Park Avenue South, New York, New York 10003.
CROWN is a trademark of Crown Publishers, Inc.

Manufactured in the United States of America

Library of Congress Cataloging-in-Publication Data
Greenfeld, Howard. Books: from writer to reader.
Bibliography: p. Includes index.
Summary: Follows a book through the various stages of publishing, printing, and marketing.
1. Books—Juvenile literature. 2. Book industries and trade—Juvenile literature. [1. Books. 2. Book industries and trade. 3. Printing] I. Title.
Z116.A2G74 1988 808′.02 88-11876

ISBN 0-517-56840-3
ISBN 0-517-56841-1 (pbk.)

2 4 6 8 10 9 7 5 3 1

First Revised Edition

CONTENTS

Acknowledgments

Special thanks are due Norma Jean Sawicki, without whom this book about books would never have become a book. I would also like to express my gratitude to John Grandits for extending the life of this book through this revised edition.

For assistance in gathering illustrations and for granting permission to reproduce them, I would like to thank the following: The Author's Guild, Lucy Bate, Jill Bennett, *Booklist,* R. R. Bowker Company, Tatyana Bylinsky, Teryl Euvremer, June Gaddy, Marvin Glass, Gail E. Haley, Halliday Lithograph Corporation, Harris Corporation, International Paper, *Kirkus Reviews,* Ralph and Terry Kovel, Lingen Verlag Köln, Giulio Maestro, The Mergenthaler Linotype Corporation, Edward Miller, Murray Printing Company, Michael Pietsch, *Publishers Weekly, School Library Journal,* Cat Bowman Smith, Society of Authors' Representatives, Hudson Talbott, Tamar Taylor, University of Chicago Press, Vandersons Corporation, White Rabbit Bookstore, Sylvie Wickstrom, Jack Ziegler.

BOOKS
FROM WRITER TO READER

INTRODUCTION

They entertain us or inform us; they make us laugh or make us cry; they please us, or they anger us. They have the extraordinary power to change the life of an individual or even the way of thinking of an entire society.

Books play a vital part in our lives. When we are young they introduce us to the world of fantasy and beauty, not only by means of words but also through illustrations. In school, they educate us, and as we grow up, their range becomes even broader. Books are essential if we want to study law or medicine or engineering—or really anything at all. If we read the right book we can learn to cook a meal or sew a dress or play chess or many other things.

Books are indeed such a fundamental part of our lives that many people take them for granted. It is impossible to imagine a world without them. They somehow appear, almost miraculously; we have them and read them and enjoy them without giving much thought to their origin.

I have spent many years in the world of books. I have written them and edited them and published them and sold them. Throughout these years, many people—those who do not take books for granted—have asked me questions: How do you write a book? What do you do with a manuscript once you've written it? What is the role of the literary agent? What does a publisher do? What is the job of the editor? How does a book get illustrated? How is it printed and how is it bound? And what can be done to see that a book finally reaches the reader?

This book is an attempt to answer these and other questions, and the answers will make it clear that the process of conceiving and making a book is a long, complicated, and difficult one. Books don't grow on trees. They are the result of teamwork, of many creative people joining together to produce a work that each hopes may, in some small way, enrich the world. It's not all idealism, of course. There are strictly commercial and business considerations involved; book publishing is, after all, a business and must be conducted as such. Yet there is something special in it, an indefinable excitement in the knowledge that each book will have a life of its own, will survive longer than other essential products—like shoes or cars or dresses—in someone's home, in a public library, or in the mind of the reader.

THE WRITER

The book inevitably begins with the writer, without whom there could be no book. The writer's job is to fill blank pieces of paper with words and sentences—the right words in the right order to convey ideas or thoughts or facts or visions or dreams to a prospective reader. No one writer is like another; they are individuals, writing for different reasons with different goals in mind. Each writer has different working habits. Some work mornings, some work afternoons, and some work at night. There are writers who can create for eight hours a day and some who can work no more than two hours a day. There are no regular routines, as in an office, and it is impossible to order a writer to work a certain number of hours per day or per week and expect that author to obey. Creation, the act of writing a book, depends on many things: on mood, on inspiration, even on the weather.

The method and place of creation, too, differ from writer to writer. Increasingly, writers make use of computers and word processors, which allow them to revise easily what they write. They can insert, delete, or move words and sentences, and see the results on a screen without having to retype entire paragraphs or pages. Some authors, however, continue to use a typewriter, while others prefer to write in longhand. Some writers need the silence of the country, some need the noise and excitement of a city. Some will write the whole book before revising and polishing the manuscript, while others prefer to work slowly and perfect each passage as they go along. There are even cases of writers who like to write standing up, although it is undoubtedly true that most prefer to do their work while sitting down.

So we see that writers differ among themselves in very many ways. A writer is not a machine, but an individual creator. His job is a difficult and often a lonely one, and when he begins his work, he cannot predict just how much he will accomplish; some days he can write ten pages with ease, and other days he is hardly able to write more than ten sentences.

The form in which writers choose to express themselves varies, too. There are men and women who write poetry or children's books, plays, works of fiction or works of nonfiction. Some write as part of a group, contributing to textbooks or encyclopedias. Of course, it is not necessary for any one author to be restricted to any single genre. Many novelists have also written plays, just as many biographers have written children's books, although each of these does require a specialized skill.

A poet is most concerned with language, with the sound and rhythm of words as well as their precise meanings. The writer of a children's book must keep the age of the reader in mind. A playwright is, of course, concerned with dialogue and with dramatic movement, the playwright's work generally

An author at a word processor

being destined for performance on a stage by actors, before an audience. In general, however, books fall into two categories: fiction and nonfiction.

Works of fiction are works of the imagination, the most common being the novel or the short story, while nonfiction includes all works of fact: biography, history, science, philosophy, and so on. For novelists, playwrights, or short story writers there are few limitations. They are free to create characters of their own choosing, settings both real and imaginary, stories both logical and illogical. These writers can write realistic books about things and people that might be familiar to all of us, or they might create, in works of fantasy, the most bizarre or unfamiliar characters and situations, totally unfamiliar to us.

Most writers of fiction begin with a character or a set of characters. They may have no plot when they begin to write—merely these characters who will be placed in certain situations. From these characters, a plot or a story will evolve. All peoples, from all times, have been interested in stories about people and in the suspense that many stories involve. A formula of universal interest might well be: How will a character or characters solve a given problem? The problem could be a murder or finding a way of life, or a complicated romantic situation, but whatever it is, it will be of interest only if the characters themselves are of interest.

Many writers are actually led by their characters, having no idea of where these characters might lead them by the time the story is completed. In a sense, the characters they create in turn create the plot. Other authors carefully plan their stories or plots before beginning the long job of writing them. They outline each development chapter by chapter; they make brief sketches of the characters for their own use; they make physical plans of a house or a town that may serve as the setting for their story.

However they work, the novelists must become deeply involved in the lives of the characters they have created. This involvement does not end during "off" hours; they are inevitably with their characters twenty-four hours a day. They become an integral part of the author's life as long as their stories are being written, and this involvement/identification begins well before the actual words are put onto paper and lasts well beyond the point at which the actual writing is finished.

A novelist or short story writer writes, above all, out of a need to write, a desire to describe the people or places, or a will to tell a given story. The writer conveys a mood, brings characters to life, creates an atmosphere of time or place, real or unreal. The successful novel involves the readers in a world other than their own, or illuminates for them parts of their own world that they have never examined. The writer's tool

Had been newspaper reporter in US and correspondent abroad.

1894 new [illegible] Frank [illegible]

Jolas – Born in US of Lorraine parents, spent childhood in L.

and returned to US at 15. Fluent in English, French + German. and wrote poetry in [illegible]

About 33 when 1st + published.

(Josephson) "a very lovable man" In spite of Josephson's opposition to JS, J appointed him contributing editor of +

Poverty in US, first made living as grocery boy in Brooklyn, reporter in Waterbury, Conn during Palmer raids. BOYLE-206

Salon in 1927-8 became a "chapel for the idolaters of J. J." (Josephson

Physical – broad-shouldered, heavy-set, fine head, wild poetic gaze
Short, dark, shiny-faced, full of verve

Maria Jolas – Tall, good-looking, from Kentucky, Statuesque, handsome MacDonald
warm, hospitable, musical, sensitive, full of enthusiasm for all forms of mod. art
Donated much money to Joyce family when he was going blind.

Jolases (Crosby) "Grand, gifted people. with minds like new brooms, hearts like hearts."

An author's notes for a biography

for this is language; words serve a writer just as colors and shapes serve a painter and notes and sounds serve a musician.

There are schools for novelists, courses in writing the novel or the short story, and these may be of some help. But no academic training can transform a student into a successful writer of fiction. Novelists or short story writers depend on their own experience and imagination, on sensitivity and the power of observation. Of course, there must be a love of and a feeling for words, for the proper language with which to express these experiences and insights into human beings. A novelist creates a world and the people in it and the situations that these people may find themselves in; there are few, if any, lessons that can be learned from study, other than—and this is essential—the reading of other books and the knowledge of how other authors may or may not have solved their problems.

Such is not the case with the writer of nonfiction—that is, biography, history, science, all works that are dependent not on the imagination but on fact. The writer of such works must be knowledgeable about the field in which he or she chooses to write, and academic training will be helpful in many cases and absolutely essential in others.

Biographers or historians or science writers will be required to spend many months or often years researching their subjects. This means an enormous amount of reading, of poring through books in libraries, of tracing facts to their original sources. While doing the research, every writer of nonfiction learns what every reader should know—that not everything found in books is necessarily true. A researcher finds what seems an often astounding number of discrepancies between one source and another. Because one book will give one date and one another, and often a third date can be found in a third

Summary of Chapter lX

On Tuesday morning Marcy woke up with another bad dream She had been in a deep well and she couldn't get out because that toad was at the top of the well and he kept grinning down at her.

Toby kept marching all over the house,beating his wooden drum, until Mama made him stay out of doors."I am going to war," he cried.I am going to be a dnummer boy."

Marcy wanted to start for Pierce's Mill immediately.It would be fun to live in an old mill with many other families.They would cook out of doors and wade in the mill-pond.It would be cool out there in the woods along Rock Creek.Marcy kept begging Mama to leave.

But Mama was undecided.She said she was going to call on Aunt Dolley and ask her opinion.Mama called the president's wife Aunt Dolley because she had known her ever since she was a small girl in Philadelphia. Of course she called her Mrs.Madison when she spoke to her--since she was the First Lady of the land.

Mama took the children with her.They walked because there were no carriages to rent as Mama would have done at any other time.

At the front door of the big white house,Mama said"Now children remember your manners.Why where is Toby?"

Toby was missing.

(Descrition of President's house and of Dolley Madison)

There were two other callers,but they had come without their children. Mrs.Livingston and Mrs.Ward had grown up in Philadephia,too.

Summary of a chapter

book, writers of nonfiction must do their best to go back to the original source, to find out the truth.

In addition to reading everything possible about the subject, the writer will often find it necessary to interview various people connected with that subject. This would include other authorities in the field, eyewitnesses to an event, or friends or acquaintances of the subject of a biography.

In the course of all this work that takes place prior to the actual writing of the book, nonfiction writers must take voluminous notes. They will distinguish their sources and choose which authorities to believe and which to doubt. They must then be selective, above all keeping in mind the audience for whom the book is intended. Obviously, a work meant for scholars will require more detail than one meant for the general reader, just as a book written for children will have to be approached differently from one written for adults.

Once the facts have been gathered, the book must be organized in the most readable, dramatic, as well as logical sequence. If the gathering and selection of factual material require scholarship and intelligence, the interpretation and organization of this material require imagination and literary skill. Many an interesting subject has been made dull by an unskilled biographer, while many less interesting figures have been made more exciting by their more gifted biographers, just as a historical event of minor importance can be made fascinating by an imaginative author.

In the end, fiction and nonfiction alike are the result of a writer's inspiration and/or interest, but it is essential to remember the writer's dedication as well. It is popular to think of a writer's life as being glamorous and romantic; however, the opposite is generally true. There is creative satisfaction involved in the writing of a book, just as there is in all creative activity, but more than that there is hard work, and every writer spends far more time writing than attending well-publicized cocktail parties. Financial sacrifice, too, is usually involved, as few writers are able to earn very much money for their work. In fact, the large majority of writers have full-time jobs to support themselves and their families and must write at night or during weekends.

But the true writer writes out of a need to express himself or herself or to inform or educate the public. It is this passion, and it is no less than that, that drives most writers to undertake the difficult task of writing a book.

It is the hope of all writers that their words will be set into type and then printed and bound, and the result, a book, will be then read by the reader. The pleasure or the insight or the knowledge that this reader will receive from the book should make the writer's struggle worthwhile.

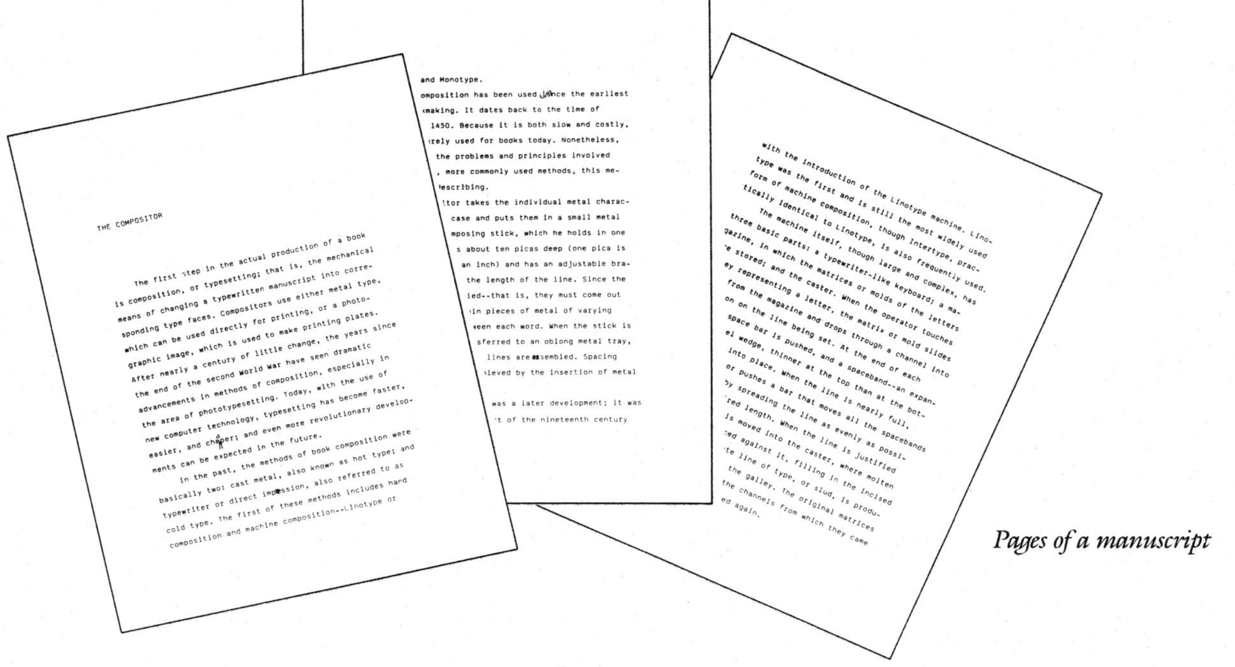

THE COMPOSITOR

The first step in the actual production of a book is composition, or typesetting; that is, the mechanical means of changing a typewritten manuscript into corresponding type faces. Compositors use either metal type, which can be used directly for printing, or a photographic image, which is used to make printing plates. After nearly a century of little change, the years since the end of the second World War have seen dramatic advancements in methods of composition, especially in the area of phototypesetting. Today, with the use of new computer technology, typesetting has become faster, easier, and cheaper; and even more revolutionary developments can be expected in the future.

In the past, the methods of book composition were basically two: cast metal, also known as hot type; and typewriter or direct impression, also referred to as cold type. The first of these methods includes hand composition and machine composition--Linotype or

and Monotype.
omposition has been used since the earliest
making. It dates back to the time of
1450. Because it is both slow and costly,
rely used for books today. Nonetheless,
the problems and principles involved
, more commonly used methods, this me-
lescribing.
tor takes the individual metal charac-
case and puts them in a small metal
mposing stick, which he holds in one
s about ten picas deep (one pica is
an inch) and has an adjustable bra-
the length of the line. Since the
ied--that is, they must come out
in pieces of metal of varying
veen each word. When the stick is
sferred to an oblong metal tray,
lines are assembled. Spacing
iieved by the insertion of metal

was a later development; it was
t of the nineteenth century

with the introduction of the Linotype machine. Linotype was the first and is still the most widely used
form of machine composition, though Intertype, practically identical to Linotype, is also frequently used.
The machine itself, though large and complex, has
three basic parts: a typewriter-like keyboard; a magazine, in which the matrices or molds of the letters
e stored; and the caster. When the operator touches
ey representing a letter, the matrix or mold slides
from the magazine and drops through a channel into
on on the line being set. At the end of each
space bar is pushed, and a spaceband--an expan-
el wedge, thinner at the top than at the bot-
into place. When the line is nearly full,
or pushes a bar that moves all the spacebands
by spreading the line as evenly as possi-
red length. When the line is justified
is moved into the caster, where molten
ed against it, filling in the incised
te line of type, or slud, is produ-
the galley. The original matrices
the channels from which they came
ed again.

Pages of a manuscript

THE LITERARY AGENT

After a great deal of work, long periods of hope, and often longer periods of despair, the writer has finished writing the book. The manuscript, having been neatly typed, double-spaced, is ready to be submitted for publication. It is at this point that many new writers feel helpless. It's obviously not enough to write the book—it must be read. And the words set down on manuscript paper by the writer cannot be read by a number of people until they are put into the form of a book and thus made suitable for reading. A publisher and only a publisher will do this.

But there are many publishers, and it is necessary to find the right one. A few writers may know someone in publishing and eagerly submit their manuscripts to their friends or acquaintances. Others may know of guides to publishing houses such as *Literary Market Place* or *Writer's Market* and select a potential publisher from among the many listed there. Still others could be among those very few readers who pay

Reference books for authors

attention to the name of a publishing house whose books seem to be similar to the ones they have written and so they send their manuscripts off to those houses.

Any of these methods may help, but at this stage the writer may want professional help, and one way he or she can obtain that help is from a literary agent.

Literary agents are scouts for talented writers and often helpful and perceptive editors. They are also in business, and the success or failure in handling the affairs of a client will determine the success or failure of the literary agency. The agent is often in the best position to know not only what is salable and what is not, but also which publisher would be best suited to publish a particular work. There are all kinds and sizes of agencies—large ones with staffs of fifty and small ones with a staff of one. Nonetheless, it is always one agent who is responsible for the work of each author, and each agent has his or her special tastes and qualifications.

The agent must always be on the lookout for new talent and be able to recognize the potentialities of young, unknown authors. At the same time agents should be willing to encourage and promote an established author's work through guidance and constructive suggestions. The agent must also be in touch with publishers, must know what is being published by each house, and the taste of each editor. Good agents are selective, knowing that their business will suffer if inferior works are offered to a publisher, just as they must be willing and able to advise the author as to ways in which a manuscript could be improved, if that manuscript shows promise. In many ways, a good agent acts as a clearinghouse for a publisher, eliminating the hopelessly bad and encouraging the good. It is for this reason that manuscripts submitted by careful agents, known for their taste and knowledge of the market, may often receive more careful attention than will a manuscript submitted by either an unknown author or an irresponsible agent.

Many writers who feel they could use the services of an agent in marketing a manuscript are with good reason puzzled as to how to find this agent. There are, however, various ways of finding a list of reputable, well-established agents: through *Literary Market Place* or *Writer's Market*; through The Authors Guild, which is an association of writers; or by consulting a list provided by an organization called the Society of Authors' Representatives. With any one of these lists on hand, the author should choose and write to one or even several agents, describing the work he wishes to submit, perhaps enclosing an outline, synopsis, or sample chapters, giving a résumé of his background and experience, and, of course, mentioning any previously published work. No full manuscript should ever be submitted to an agent before that agent requests it; many

18 Colorado/Bylinsky

As Papa dragged Frank out the door, Mama ran after them. All three rushed down the street.

Mama kept yelling, "Hurry up, hurry up!" Far down the road she turned around and ran back.

Loud voices sounded at the front door. Mama walked in, holding Aunt Peppina by the hand.

My heart was beating fast. Joe was all the way in Trinidad!

"Maybe he'll be hypnotized and he won't remember who we are," Mary said to Mama.

"Joe will be back. Go to sleep now," Mama said.

We sat in bed. Mama and Aunt Peppina were in the kitchen.

"That Frank, how could he leave his brother and my Pee Wee? He let them run off with the hypnotist!" Aunt Peppina said. "Pee Wee, Pee Wee, he doesn't know better, but Frank should have more sense!"

Mama was twisting a cotton dish rag in her hands. Her voice was shaking. "Those stupid boys," Mama said.

Aunt Peppina stood by the window. "Here they come," she said as she opened the door. Uncle Bruno and Papa walked in.

"The sheriff is going with Frank to Trinidad to find those boys...they should be back later tonight," said Uncle Bruno. His voice was deep.

Mary whispered to me. "A quarter isn't worth all the trouble."

An unedited manuscript page

agencies are unwilling or unable to take on new clients, and sending the manuscript itself before it has been requested is a waste of both time and money. In any case, although an author might write a letter of inquiry to several agents at once, he should never submit a work to more than one agent at a time.

Once the agent has shown interest in a work, he or she will, in most cases, read that work without charging the author a fee. There are some agents, however, who do charge a reading fee for each manuscript submitted and others who charge what they call an editorial fee. The former might be justified on the grounds that an agent spends a large amount of time reading works that might never be salable, and should be paid for that time. The editorial fee, however, for which an agent promises to edit a manuscript so that it might be suitable for a submission to a publisher, is not justifiable. The author's manuscript should be edited by the editor at the publishing house that undertakes to publish it and not by an agent—although there is no harm and sometimes benefit from an agent's suggestions once that agent has agreed to handle the manuscript. This, however, is part of the agent's job, one for which there should be no charge. A writer must realize that, just as there are good and bad writers, there are also good and bad agents.

Once the writer has found an agent who is willing to submit the manuscript to a publisher, the relationship between writer and agent can be very close. It is, of course, best that the writer understand just what can and cannot be expected of the agent.

The agent reads and evaluates the manuscript on hand, and on the basis of this evaluation submits the manuscript to the publisher who in the agent's judgment is best suited to publish it. Editors move from house to house, and the agent must keep up to date with these changes and with the special taste of each editor. The agent must know which editor would be most sympathetic to the work of any given writer, and to that writer's personality. Markets, too, change, and an agent should be aware of these changes, of trends, and of fashions.

Once the manuscript has been accepted for publication, the agent must perform the complicated task of negotiating the contract. The agent must know realistically what to expect both as an advance—which will be paid to the author against future royalty—and as royalty. Asking for too large an advance or too high a royalty percentage might well lose a sale. This is part of the good business sense essential in an agent, for the agent represents the author in all business dealings with the publisher.

As part of the contract, too, the agent will most probably take on certain responsibilities by retaining specified rights on behalf of the author and trying to sell them on behalf of the

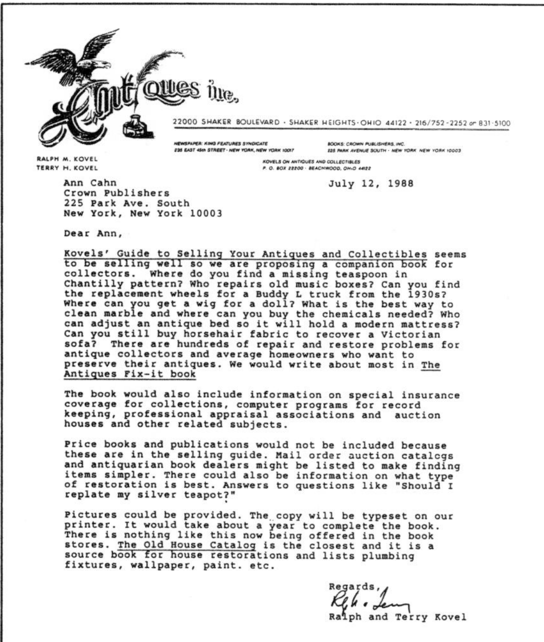

Antiques Inc.

22000 SHAKER BOULEVARD · SHAKER HEIGHTS · OHIO 44122 · 216/752-2252 or 831-5100

NEWSPAPER: KING FEATURES SYNDICATE
235 EAST 45th STREET · NEW YORK, NEW YORK 10017

BOOKS: CROWN PUBLISHERS, INC.
225 PARK AVENUE SOUTH · NEW YORK NEW YORK 10003

KOVELS ON ANTIQUES AND COLLECTIBLES
P. O. BOX 22200 · BEACHWOOD, OHIO 44122

RALPH M. KOVEL
TERRY H. KOVEL

Ann Cahn
Crown Publishers
225 Park Ave. South
New York, New York 10003

July 12, 1988

Dear Ann,

Kovels' Guide to Selling Your Antiques and Collectibles seems to be selling well so we are proposing a companion book for collectors. Where do you find a missing teaspoon in Chantilly pattern? Who repairs old music boxes? Can you find the replacement wheels for a Buddy L truck from the 1930s? Where can you get a wig for a doll? What is the best way to clean marble and where can you buy the chemicals needed? Who can adjust an antique bed so it will hold a modern mattress? Can you still buy horsehair fabric to recover a Victorian sofa? There are hundreds of repair and restore problems for antique collectors and average homeowners who want to preserve their antiques. We would write about most in The Antiques Fix-it book

The book would also include information on special insurance coverage for collections, computer programs for record keeping, professional appraisal associations and auction houses and other related subjects.

Price books and publications would not be included because these are in the selling guide. Mail order auction catalogs and antiquarian book dealers might be listed to make finding items simpler. There could also be information on what type of restoration is best. Answers to questions like "Should I replate my silver teapot?"

Pictures could be provided. The copy will be typeset on our printer. It would take about a year to complete the book. There is nothing like this now being offered in the book stores. The Old House Catalog is the closest and it is a source book for house restorations and lists plumbing fixtures, wallpaper, paint. etc.

Regards,

Ralph and Terry Kovel

A book proposal

ROYALTY STATEMENT

For the period 3/1/75 through 8/31/75

AUTHOR: PAYABLE TO:

TITLE:

RETAIL PRICE: $4.50

REGULAR TRADE SALES:					
6,501	copies sold at a royalty of	5% of	4.50	$ 1,462.73
	copies sold at a royalty of	% of		
	copies sold at a royalty of	% of		
RETAIL SALES:				
	copies sold at a royalty of	% of		
SPECIAL and FOREIGN SALES:				
1,100	copies sold at a royalty of	5% of	2.25	123.75
311	copies sold at a royalty of	2½% of	4.50	34.99
50	copies sold at a royalty of	5% of	1.80	4.50
200	copies sold at a royalty of	5% of	2.43	24.30

TOTAL ROYALTIES: $ 1,650.27

OTHER INCOME:

Book Club Rights Weekly Reader 3/24/75	$	1,625.00
Reprint Rights		
British Empire Income		
Translation Rights		
Permissions Granted		

TOTAL OTHER INCOME:

TOTAL ROYALTIES and OTHER INCOME: $ 3,275.27

DEDUCTIONS:

Advance Royalty	$
Sundry Charges	
Book Purchases	
Unearned Balance From Previous Statement	

TOTAL DEDUCTIONS:

TOTAL EARNINGS DUE: $ 3,275.27

A royalty statement

agency. These rights include dramatic rights, for radio, television, motion-picture, or theatrical adaptation; first serial rights, that is, rights to print parts, or even the whole, of a book in a magazine before the book is actually published; and, because most agents have representatives or affiliates in foreign countries, rights to publish the book either in another language or in another English-speaking country. Disposing of these rights can involve a great deal of work, but it can be most profitable for the agent as well as for the author.

The agent collects all the money—whether from the publishing house or other sources—that the author earns from the book and passes it on to the author, after deducting the agent's commission, which is almost always 10 or 15 percent of the total amount earned by the author. This arrangement lasts as long as the work brings in money—even if the author and agent have in the meantime separated. The agent, too, examines royalty statements, requesting corrections when necessary, and often checks on the publisher's handling of the book in its various stages of publication as well as after that, seeing to it that the book is properly published and sold.

There are limitations, however, to what agents can or should do. They cannot sell an unsalable work—no agent can be expected to perform miracles. An agent, though helpful editorially at times, is not an editor and thus cannot be expected to edit a manuscript or teach a writer how to write. Nor can an agent be asked to spend too much time on any single client. An author, deeply involved in his own work, may mistakenly believe that he is the agent's only, or, at least, most important, client. This is obviously not the case, and just as an agent must understand the author's needs, that author must understand the agent's limitations. With both parties keeping that in mind, their relationship can be a rewarding and mutually beneficial one.

THE PUBLISHING HOUSE

With the help of a literary agent, or without it (beginning authors are often unable to find agents willing to represent them), the manuscript's next destination is a publishing house. There the decision to publish or not to publish will be made. If that decision is a positive one, it is the responsibility of the publishing house to bring the work to the public. For this reason, it is most helpful for the author to have some idea of the structure of that hard-to-define organization and its workings.

Harmony

Warner

A publishing house is made up of a group of variously creative people working together to produce and sell books. Ideally, each book will be a different and unique product that will prove both valuable artistically and profitable commercially. These two goals are of equal importance, and although they sometimes come into conflict, neither can be forgotten in the long and complicated process of publishing a book.

No two publishing houses are the same, and each acquires,

through the list of books it publishes, a special character. They differ in size, too; there are small houses that have a staff of three people, and there are large houses with hundreds of people. Basically, however, they must all perform the same functions, and thus are divided into similar departments.

The publisher is the overall director, whose spirit and interests should guide the policy of the house and who coordinates the work of the various departments. Publishers neither write books nor print them. They buy writing and pay for the making of books and then sell them. They are ultimately responsible for the books selected and for the manner in which they are published.

There are basically two kinds of publishers. One might be called the corporate publisher, whose chief concern is business and efficiency. The other is the personal publisher, one whose individual taste is strongly reflected in the nature of the books presented to the public and who is somewhat more concerned with artistic values than with business. Profit and loss, though, are as much part of a personal publishing house as they are of the corporate kind. Ideally, the personal publisher is a person whose courage and vision bring to the reader works of daring and originality, often works ahead of their time. In the past these publishers made major contributions to literature. Today, more and more small houses are being bought by huge corporations, many (but not all) concerned far less with literature than with profit. But just as some small, good houses are absorbed, other small, personal publishers are taking their places. These small houses need both courage and money to found what is inevitably a very difficult business, one that is slow to build. However, no matter how great the risks, new publishers will be born as long as there are men and women devoted to the beauty and power of the book.

Vintage

Villard

Alfred A. Knopf

American Geographic

Clarkson N. Potter

Random House

Orion

Schocken

This is not to say that the large publisher cannot be a positive and valuable force in American publishing. Corporate publishers have the resources to produce economically a wide variety of titles and distribute them around the world. It is to be hoped that both large and small publishers will continue to survive and prosper.

Publishers, no matter how gifted, cannot work alone. They are inevitably dependent on those men and women who work with them in the various departments of the publishing house. These departments generally include: the editorial department; art, design, and production; and publicity, sales, promotion, and advertising. The first two are concerned largely with the making of the book, its preparation and manufacture. The other departments mentioned are concerned largely with doing everything possible to see that any given book is promoted and sold.

In addition, there is the business department, which is concerned with paying bills for work done and making and collecting invoices for books sold, as well as the shipping department, which must see that books reach their destination.

All of these many parts of a publishing house work together and cooperate through the many stages that lead to the publication of a book. They frequently consult and advise one another, and all of their efforts should be carefully coordinated. For this reason, it is useful for members of each department to have at least some understanding of the work done in other departments. An editor with a knowledge of the problems of book production is far more valuable than an editor who knows nothing about the actual manufacturing of a book. By the same token, the production department should be aware of the problems facing the sales department, just as the publicity department must keep in contact with the editorial department, and so on.

A publishing house draws upon a large variety of creative skills—literary, artistic, technical, promotional, and commercial. All of these must come together, since each book is the result of the common effort of many people, each of whom has a different talent and skill. As with any group of people working together, there are bound to be differences of opinion, honest differences of judgment as to what method would bring about the best result. These disagreements concern what books are to be published, how much is to be spent on their manufacture, and in what ways they might best be publicized and, finally, sold. These differences, far from harming a book or its sales, should really improve them by stimulating all efforts toward turning out the best possible book in the most economically sound way.

Pantheon

THE DECISION TO PUBLISH

The first important decision to be made in a publishing house is to select, from the large number of manuscripts submitted, those that will be accepted for publication. It is most often a very difficult decision, and very many factors are involved in making it.

Book publishing is a uniquely complex field. The publisher is often torn between the obligation to publish works of literary merit and the necessity to sell enough copies of any given book to make enough money to continue to publish more books. Publishing is a business, and must be run as a business in order to survive. Publishers must show a financial profit just as any business must. On the other hand, it differs from most businesses in that the publisher has a moral duty to see that works of artistic or educational value—even those that have but a small chance of being commercially successful—are made available to the public. The publishers of the early work of some of the greatest writers of our time, James Joyce and

William Faulkner, for example, knew that these books would not be financially profitable in the beginning. Yet they published them in the hope that they would sell over a long period of time.

The decision whether or not to publish a book is made in many different ways, depending on the size of the publishing house, its economic structure, the nature of its list, and the makeup of its staff.

In some cases, a single enthusiastic editor or publisher, carried away by the merits of a manuscript, will fight to see that the work is accepted. In other cases, an editorial board consisting of several editors, each of whom has read the manuscript, might discuss the pros and cons at an editorial meeting and then reach a decision. Or the manuscript might be submitted to the sales department, and the opinion of the sales force as to the book's commercial value might be the decisive factor.

Fiction and nonfiction will be judged in different ways. A novel, a play, poetry, or a collection of short stories is more likely to be accepted on the basis of the work's literary merit and the publisher's feelings about the author's potential to write more books in the future. Often an editor might say that although a first novel is flawed, the author shows such superior talent that the book is worth publishing in order to encourage that author to go on to write more books—for the same publisher, of course. In a business sense, that author becomes an investment for the future. Indeed, many writers whose first novels have failed commercially have gone on to become best-selling, or at least commercially successful, authors in later years.

When it comes to the decision regarding a work of nonfiction, the publishing house has at its disposal certain facts that

to each section.

Anyway, I love this stuff. A lot of other writers and reviewers do too. Da Capo has lined up lots of support for its reissue. Because of his local following and because lots of people hate LA, this should do well in California. Sandy and Howie like the idea. And we should be able to sell some outside LA because lots of people love Meltzer's writing.

So what do you think?

Michael

3/20/87

Esther,

Here's a proposal so strange I think it has to be right for us.

Richard Meltzer is revered among some of us rock 'n' rollers as one of the greatest writers the music has ever had. His irreverence and refusal to like something just because everyone else ~~seemed to~~ did made him one of the freshest voices there was. His book THE AESTHETICS OF ROCK is a classic, just about to be reissued by Da Capo.

He expanded from Rock to Culture: his book GULCHER (Straight Arrow '72) is a hilarious, bizarre miscellany.

So is his new book. Meltzer has lived in Los Angeles for the last ten years. He hates it, but it's perfect: as he says, since it's noplace it makes the perfect office.

His articles in the READER, L.A. WEEKLY, and other local papers, plus gigs on radio and public access tv, have made him a local cult hero. He writes his unique rants on apparently whatever comes to mind. But they're all about Los Angeles to some extent, even when on the surface they're about love, sports, tv or food.

A DIVISION OF CROWN PUBLISHERS, INC.
225 PARK AVENUE SOUTH, NEW YORK, NEW YORK 10003
(212) 254-1600 · TELEX 427195

The book is a thematic collection of these pieces, with new intros

A reader's comments on a proposal

will make the decision an easier one. For example, a travel book on Italy might be submitted to a publisher who examines it and finds it both well written and informative. That's not enough, however. The publisher must find out how many travel books about Italy have been published, how many are still in print—that is, available to the public—how well they have sold or are selling, just how the manuscript under consideration differs from these other books, and how much knowledge and information the manuscript in question adds to those already published. In other words, publishers must determine how much interest there is in the subject and must ask themselves why a reader would buy this book rather than any of the other books available.

In back of each publisher's mind there must always be those two questions of artistic and financial responsibility. The decision to publish a book is a commitment of much money, time, and effort. Because of this, before offering a contract to an author, it is often essential to have at least a rough idea of just how a book will be manufactured and how much it will cost. The more information the publisher has, the easier it will be to come to a decision; the facts determined in advance can also serve as the basis for the terms of an eventual contract.

For each projected book, the publisher should bear in mind just what the retail price of the book should be. This is determined on the basis of probable costs of manufacture as well as the prices of similar books meant for the same market. For example, if the length of the book and the material to be included in it are such that it would have to bear an unusually high retail price, the publisher, before agreeing to publish the book, must be certain that there actually is a market for such a book at so high a price.

These conclusions are relatively easy to reach. Probable

cost can be roughly estimated by past experience with books of similar length and types of material to be included, such as illustrations. Prices of similar books on the market can be easily determined through a survey made by the sales department—or, for that matter, by anyone who carefully browses through a bookstore. There are some things that a publisher knows from experience: a medium-length novel must be priced competitively with similar novels; an illustrated biography or work of history can be sold for a higher price than the novel could; a highly specialized work meant for a limited public (which will, out of necessity, buy the book at almost any price) is able to carry a high retail price. The publisher knows, too, that a high retail price can even be advantageous in the case of what is essentially a gift book, a lavishly illustrated volume that is often called a coffee table book since it is frequently shown off—on a coffee table—rather than read.

Retail price will depend, too, on the number of copies to be printed, a projection that can be made by the sales and editorial departments. While it is true that the more copies printed the less each single copy of a book will cost, it would be foolish to print a large number of copies of a title merely to bring the retail price down when it is clear that that number of copies cannot be sold. It makes no sense to produce ten thousand copies of a book in order to obtain a low cost, when only five thousand can reasonably be expected to sell. In addition, because of increasing inventory costs—the cost of holding unsold books in the warehouse—publishers must determine how many copies can be sold over a given period of time. A first printing will often be based on projected sales over a twelve- to eighteen-month period.

This decision is an extremely important one, and whenever possible should be determined in advance. It is here that

Be sure to list name of supplier for all manufacturing

PLANT COST BO____ List____ BB____

C AA's/EA's____
O Text____
P Capts. Typesetting
Index, rh, heads, misc. 1000
Display____
Cop Ed & Prfrd____
Jkt. fronts & flaps____

A Text design dummy____
R Text mech.____
T Design, dummy, mech. Jacket & Insert Freelance #1000

P Camera & Plates____
R Strip illus.____
E Make Ready 1650
P Shoot line & ____
Jkt. prep. proof____
Jkt. final pl. & blue____
Cov.____
Color seps. & pfs.____
Insert Strip & pl. Extra 110 proofs for Sales 4000
Stats & blues Conf 1500

PRE PRODUCTION ESTIMATE
Editor
Stark
Prashker
Porter
Gillis
Fagan
Alcader

M Dies____
I
S Slipcase/Box/Mech. Bds.____
C Other____

TOTAL PLANT____

S Text paper____
H Text pw____
E
E Insert paper____
T Insert pw____

C End pw & stock____
O
S Jkt. pw & stock____
T Cov. pw & stock____
Component Sheet } freight____
FOB Avenel____
TOTAL MFG. COST____
Storage____
List entire rate: ROYALTY RATE 10%
TOTAL COST____
Break even:____

Ptg #: 1 Impt: ____ ISBN #: ____ DATE ____
W.F. #: (PPE) OK Mach.____ Final____ From ____
Title: Bo... Girls (RLB)
Price: Cloth see below Paper____
Trim ____ Text Pages 32 Forms____
Insert # Pages____ Forms____
Halftones____ # Seps____
Text # Colors 4/4 Line____
Paper____ Imposition____
125 gsm Nivis Matte
Paper stocked:____ on hand:____ Must buy:____ Same as before:____
Stock size actually needed____
Waste: Quote____ Scale____ Average %____ Paper Price figured as: net +____
____ M____ Sheets____
____ M____ Sheets____
____ M____ Sheets____
Binding Specs Last bound at Bindery____
Case & Mtls. ____ w/ ____
On hand: Jkts____ Inserts____
Sewing____ Inside bulk____ Covers____
Ends____ Lining Up:____
Boards 2.5 pts. Text # Page/Sig____
Illustrations Bind As____ Back Flat Bands____

REQUEST FOR JUVENILE ESTIMATE

Date: 6/19/86
Pre-Contract ✓ Contract:____
Pub Date: Spring '87

TITLE Bossyboots – RLB
Trim 10¼" x 8" Pages 32
Author Name: David Cox
Manuscript due In
(Illustrator)/Photographer Name: David Cox
~~Art~~ Film due Oct '86
Royalty: Author $ 8% ~~Photographer/Illustrator$~~ 0
Binding Type RLB Price 8.95 Quantity 10,000 ISBN 564912
Binding Type____ Price____ Quantity____ ISBN____

SPECS:
Comp (Mss pages/kind of copy/similar books Light, 2 Lines/pg
Illustrations (describe) 4 color / Supplied Film
Printer/Separator: Top quality____ Average Quality____
Paper: color/weight finish: White / 80# / COATED Offset
Paper similar to:____
Similar book:____
Ends: Self ✓ ~~Extra~~____ Printed: one side____ both sides 0
Additional specs (describe): Headbands, case stamping, die-cut, fold-out, popups:
3 piece binding – Stamp Spine Only – one foil

EXPENSE AGAINST PRODUCTION (all non-advance/royalty costs):
Editorial: no
Art (Photo/illus for tx and jkt): no
Design (specify what jk and text stages fees include): mechanical fees
Promo/Sales Materials: we will buy

Preliminary estimate (top) *and request for estimate* (bottom)

the greatest risks in publishing a book occur, and at this point that a publisher's knowledge of the market is of greatest importance. No publisher is always right, no matter how good his instincts or advice, but as good a guess as possible must be made on the basis of previous experience with similar books, or books by the same author, as well as on a publishing house's judgment of a book's commercial appeal. It is a tricky decision, and it might well be revised before a book is actually published. Today the public may be interested in astrology, for example, but by the time the book on astrology is published the public's interest could have waned, or else there might already be too many competing books on the same subject. Readers' interests change, and most publishers are eager to follow trends. All too often, a publisher will commission or sign up a book on a subject that seems appealing, only to find, several months later when the book is ready to be sold, that several other volumes on the same subject have already appeared or are about to appear. No publisher, no sales or editorial department can be sure that a given number of copies of any title should be printed. Determination of the size of the printing is a guess based on experience and intuition of the needs of the reader; the commercial success or failure of any book depends to a great extent on the accuracy of that guess.

Other basic decisions can, at least tentatively, be made before a publisher finally agrees to publish a book. These decisions will concern the manner in which the book will be physically presented—thus affecting cost and retail price. The "trim size," the size of the book page, can be determined through the nature of the material. Costs as well as esthetics must be constantly kept in mind while making this decision. An average novel or small work of nonfiction will usually have a somewhat smaller trim size than will a larger novel or a large work of nonfiction, and a major work of nonfiction or a book that is to be heavily illustrated may be even larger. There are more or less standard sizes that will apply to most books, but there are also very many exceptions to these rules, above all for children's books, art books, and those coffee table books whose appeal might be enhanced by an unusual size.

A book can be any size that the publisher wants it to be, and a special or unusual format could be an attractive selling point, but all concerned must realize that an unusual format may raise the price of a book. It is clearly advisable to determine well in advance whether or not this novel presentation of a volume will be worthwhile.

Another factor that could weigh heavily on a publishing house's decision, both on whether to accept the book and on the eventual contract terms if that book is accepted, is the need for illustrations and the nature of the illustrations. Illustrations are expensive, whether they be original artwork or photographs. Once the original cost of their procurement has been paid, they are expensive to reproduce. This is especially true in the case of color illustrations. The use of color rather than black and white can drastically alter the cost of a book and thus its retail price. Because of this, a publisher must take great care in deciding just how many illustrations—color, and black and white—are necessary for any given book and how many can be allowed. If a book absolutely needs a certain number of illustrations and the costs involved in reproducing and printing these illustrations are excessive, the publisher will either have to reject the book or adjust the terms of the contract.

By the same token, a publisher must take into consideration costs of translation for a work not originally written in the English language. These costs are high—justifiably so, since

German edition of Books: From Writer to Reader

translation is a difficult and time-consuming job—and because of them a publisher could be forced either to reject a book or to offer the author a lower royalty scale.

Obviously, many factors are involved in deciding whether or not a manuscript should be accepted for publication, just as special factors must be taken into consideration when offering terms for a contract. Fortunately, for the author, each publisher can reach different conclusions, so that a manuscript may be rejected by several houses and still taken on by another.

Once the publisher has decided to take on a work, a contract is offered to the author or the author's agent, or sometimes to a qualified lawyer. This rather complicated agreement binds the author to the publisher, setting the rules that will be followed by both parties as long as the book is in print.

A contract to publish a book is a long document, far too

involved according to some authors, yet it is undoubtedly better to have more, rather than fewer, rules carefully defined. In this way, misunderstandings are more easily avoided.

Briefly, a contract defines the commitments to be taken by both the author and the publisher, and it establishes the financial terms therein.

Under the terms of the agreement, the author grants to the publisher the exclusive right to publish the work over a set period of time within a given territory. In return for this right, the publisher in almost all cases pays the author an advance—a guarantee—against a royalty. A royalty is a percentage of the retail price of the book. In other words, the publisher might pay an author an advance of $5,000 against a royalty of 10 percent for a certain number of copies sold, 12½ percent for a fixed number of additional copies sold, and 15 percent for any copies sold above that number. The advance is "against" royalty: for example, if the publisher has paid an advance of $5,000, the author receives no further payment until that amount has been earned from his royalties. If the book sells for $20, he receives $2 for each book sold, so that no more money is due to him until the book sells 2,500 copies. After that, he receives $2 for each copy sold, until he reaches a sale of, say, 5,000 copies. At that point, his royalty—or percentage—increases to 12½ percent, and he begins earning $2.50 for each copy sold. When he reaches a sale of, say, 10,000 copies, that percentage goes up to 15 percent of the retail price, or $3 for each copy sold.

It is important that an author understand that the financial division between author and publisher is not out of proportion, as it might seem. The publisher spends a great deal of money editing, manufacturing, promoting, and selling a book; in addition, each book is sold to stores at a discount—

Contract

AGREEMENT made the day of , 19

between , whose

address is hereinafter

referred to as the "Author," and

of 225 Park Avenue South, New York, New York, hereinafter referred to as the "Publisher," with respect to the work tentatively entitled

hereinafter referred to as the "Work."

1. The Author hereby grants to the Publisher, its successors and assigns, during the term of the copyrights in the Work and all renewals and extensions thereof as presently in force or as hereafter amended by law:

(a) The exclusive right to print, publish and sell the Work and to cause the Work to be printed, published and sold in book form in the English language in the United States of America, its present territories and possessions, Canada, and in every country throughout the world;

(b) The exclusive right to publish or license the work for publication in the English language in any country which is part of the (British) Commonwealth of Nations (exclusive of Canada); but if the Work has not been so published or licensed for publication or is not under option for such publication within eighteen (18) months after first publication of the Work in the United States in any such country, then, with respect to such country the Author may rescind the right granted in this subdivision (b), by written notice delivered to the Publisher;

(c) The exclusive right to license the Work for publication in any other language throughout the world, but as to each country and language in which the Work has not been so licensed for publication, or is not under option for such publication within three (3) years after first publication of the Work in the United States, the Author may rescind by written notice to the Publisher the right granted as to such country and language included in this subdivision (c).

2. The Author warrants that neither the Work nor any part thereof is in the public domain, that he is the sole author of the Work, and the owner of all the rights in this agreement granted to the Publisher or in which the Publisher has an interest hereunder and has full power and authority to enter into this agreement; that the Work is original with the Author in every respect; that neither the Work nor any part thereof has heretofore been published except as follows (here include permissions acquired by the Author for the Work, if any):

that the Author has not heretofore granted any rights in the Work or any part thereof except as hereinabove set forth and as follows:

With respect to any rights reserved by the Author, the Author agrees that he will notify the Publisher promptly in writing of any arrangement that he may make in connection with the Work prior to the first publication of the Work hereunder, and secure copyright protection therefore in the United States, Canada, and such other countries in which the Work may be published, and will also notify the Publisher of all copyrights in the Work or any part thereof that may hereafter be secured and will deliver to the Publisher timely, recordable assignments to the Publisher of all such United States copyrights. Prior publication of the Work and of any part thereof in any form shall be licensed by the Author only with the written consent of the Publisher. The Author agrees not to exercise any rights or commit any acts that will adversely affect any of the rights granted to the Publisher hereunder.

3. The Author warrants that the Work does not infringe any copyright or violate any other right of any person or party whatsoever and does not contain any defamatory, libelous or unlawful matter including invasions of the right of privacy or publicity of another. The Author agrees to hold the Publisher harmless against any loss, damage, expense (including legal fees), judgments and decrees which the Publisher may suffer or incur as the result of the assertion of any claim or the commencement of any action or proceeding against the Publisher upon the ground that the Work contains any defamatory, libelous or other unlawful matter which may or may not be listed above or infringes upon any copyright or violates any other right of any person or party whatsoever, or as a result of undertaking the defense of any such claim, action or proceeding against any of the Publisher's licensees or purchasers of the Work, and the payment of any judgment rendered therein, or any settlement therefor, if any. In the event that there is asserted any such claim, or an action or proceeding is instituted, the Publisher shall promptly notify the Author and may withhold payments due him under this or any other agreement with the Publisher until payment or satisfaction of the claim, judgment, or settlement is effected.

4. The Author shall deliver to the Publisher not later than months after the date of this agreement a legible typewritten or printed copy of the Work, in form and substance satisfactory and acceptable to the Publisher, complete and ready for the printer, together with material from which such illustrations, maps and diagrams as the parties may jointly deem necessary can be reproduced without redrawing for use in the volume herein

If the Publisher shall decide at any time after two years subsequent to the date of first lication of the Work that the Work is no longer salable in any edition, and no longer lends f to exploitation of the rights and powers granted it hereunder, the Publisher shall give ten notice to the Author of its intention to discontinue exploitation of the Work, in which it the Author shall have the right to terminate this agreement by giving written notice eof to the Publisher, subject to extant rights of others in the Work.

In any of the foregoing events, such notice must be given to the Publisher within sixty days after the occurrence of such event; the Author shall have the right to include in such ce of termination a statement electing to purchase (within a period of sixty [60] days after giving of such notice) the remaining copies or the films or plates of the Work (if available), oth. If he shall include such a statement, the price shall be a sum agreed upon between the hor and the Publisher, or if they shall fail to agree, than the price shall be the fair market ie thereof as determined by an arbitration conducted in the County and State of New York he American Arbitration Association under its rules applicable to commercial disputes. If Author shall fail to purchase film or plates, the Publisher shall have the right to melt film ell them as scrap or otherwise dispose of them, and if the Author shall not purchase the k, the Publisher may sell the same in the regular course of business or at the best price inable therefore, without payment to the Author of any royalty thereon. In the event of termination, if the copyright in the Work shall be in the name of the Publisher, then the lisher or its successors in interest shall assign said copyright to the Author or to the record ier of the copyright, as the case may be; and all rights then in the Publisher and thereafter quired by the Publisher shall be assigned, subject to the Publisher's right to sell its stock on d as above set forth and to receive its share of all sums due and to become due from its nsees hereunder.

17. All communications and notices hereunder (except notices of recission, breach and iination, which must be given by registered mail) may be given by ordinary mail and shall iddressed to the parties at their addresses first hereinabove set forth, or at such other ress as either party may designate in a notice given to the other party.

18. This agreement contains the full agreement of the parties and all representations, ranties and inducements made by either of them, and may not be changed orally; and no lification thereof nor any waiver of any term thereof shall be valid unless it be in writing ed by both the Publisher and the Author.

19. This agreement shall be binding upon and inure to the benefit of the successors and gns of the Author and the successors and assigns of the Publisher.

20. The Author hereby empowers the Publisher to pay his agent, all monies become due under this agreement and declares that the said agent's receipts shall be a l and valid discharge. The Author further empowers the Publisher to treat with said agent ll matters arising out of this agreement, by which the Author shall be bound.

WITNESS the signature of the Author, and of the Publisher by its duly authorized officer.

....
Author

.................................L.S.

By

....

Contract

FOR THE PUBLICATION OF

between

and

Agent

Dated

A standard contract

the store too must make a profit—and this discount averages approximately 43 percent of the retail price.

In addition to the royalty paid to the author on the number of books sold, the publisher agrees to pay the author a certain percentage of other rights, called subsidiary rights. However, if the author is represented by an agent, the agent will keep some of these rights. Subsidiary rights include sales to paperback houses for inexpensive reprint, rights to excerpt in textbooks and anthologies, book club rights, movie and television rights, translations into foreign languages, serialization in newspapers and magazines, and many more.

Most important, of course, the publisher through this contract agrees to print and publish the work in the best possible way, while the author guarantees that the work is his or her own and agrees to furnish all material necessary to the completion of the book—a bibliography, an index, a glossary, and so on, if any of these is required.

This is the beginning of a partnership between author and publisher. They will be working together, and it is in the interest of both parties that the book be published well and successfully—that the author's aims in writing the book be faithfully carried out in its manufacture and presentation, and that the largest possible number of copies be sold. As with any business partnership, however, these complicated and detailed rules must be established at the beginning, and the responsibilities of each partner defined as clearly as possible before the actual partnership becomes effective.

THE EDITOR

When an author's manuscript is accepted for publication, it is assigned to an editor—in most cases the person who acquired the manuscript for the publishing house. At that point, it is the editor's function to work with that manuscript and that author. Editors become the authors' intermediary between the work they have done by themselves and the public they hope to reach.

Nonetheless, editors do more than merely edit. Above all they must be in close touch with what is being written—not only in the United States but throughout the world. They must read newspapers and magazines, getting from them ideas for books. They must keep their eyes open for new talent, reading short stories wherever they appear as a possible lead to a new and promising author. A good short story published in a magazine by a previously unknown writer will almost always bring a letter from a book editor, asking to see more of the author's work, in the hopes that a book could develop. The editor discovers talent and encourages it wherever it might be found.

Editors must keep in contact with literary agents, obtaining from them the works of their most promising authors. They solicit manuscripts and read and evaluate all those that come to their attention, unsolicited as well as solicited. Their job does not end when they leave their offices; they are constantly on the lookout for new books and new ideas and, in the case of an idea that seems suitable for a book, they must be able to find the proper author to write that book. Commissioned books, which develop from an idea born in a publishing house, often make up a substantial part of a publisher's list, and it is largely the task of the editors to come up with such ideas.

All of this is important, yet the editor's main job is to edit, and the relationship between editor and author, at least in the several months preceding publication of the book, is a very special and close one. The author has been alone with his manuscript for months or even years. It might have been shown to a wife or husband or friend, but it is most likely that no one has read it as critically, as closely, or as objectively as the editor will. Indeed, if the editors do their jobs well, they must absorb every part of that manuscript and give it their most careful and sympathetic attention.

Obviously, the role of the editor is an extremely important one in the making of a book and it must not be underestimated. Nor, on the other hand, should it be overestimated. It is romantic to read of an editor acting as a constant companion, a kind of psychoanalyst to an author, but this rarely happens. The editor is a professional aid, but not more than that. There have been relationships between editors and authors that have become legends. Such and such author, we hear, could never have written as well had it not been for a sensitive editor who held the author's hand during nights of insomnia or rescued a writer from lengthy drinking bouts, and so on. Undoubtedly, some editors have established unusually close and personal relationships with some authors, but editors cannot "make" authors a success, just as they happily lack the power to make them a failure.

The editor's main responsibility is to work on manuscripts as a constructive critic. Once the "finished" manuscript is in the hands of an editor, the author will realize that the manuscript might not really be finished and that a considerable amount of rewriting or polishing might still be necessary—with the help of the editor. Editors look for ways in which manuscripts could be improved. They suggest changes, but they will not make them themselves—they are not writers. In the end, intelligent editors know that the author's wishes must be respected—for the book will, after all, be published under the name of the author, who is the one to assume final responsibility—but that their important function is to offer guidance when necessary.

Editors work in many ways, but most probably they will begin by reading the typewritten manuscript as a whole to get an overall picture of the work. It should be noted that today many publishing houses allow an author to turn in an electronic manuscript, one which has been written on a word processor or computer. In this case, the copy is on a floppy disk rather than on paper, but for convenience in reading it is essential that the author also submit the entire manuscript printed out on paper. When the editor is ready to begin editing, the disk can be put into the editor's computer and all the work done right on the disk. By using a modem—a telephone connection between computers—the editor and

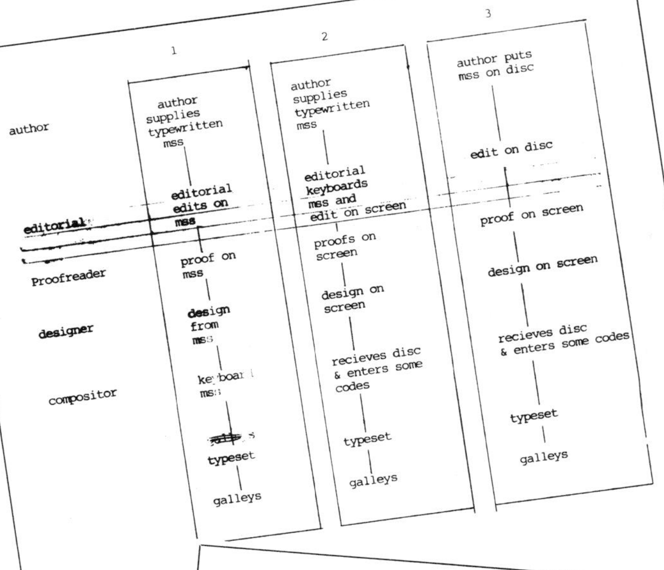

CROWN PUBLISHERS Inc.

21 Aug 87

Howard Greenfeld

Dear Howard,

I've read the chapters you've sent in and they look great. I'm going over them right now and I'll be in touch with any comments.

I'm enclosing the composition chapter. This was a tough one. I've made quite a few comments on the existing chapter. I am also suppling new material. The chapter should be organized as follows (I think):

The Compositor

Intro
Hot metal systems
hand set
Linotype/Intertype (I cut some)
Monotype (I've cut a lot)
Ludlow (I rec that we delete. No one uses it anymore)
Cold type (I've cut some. You may want to cut more)
Photo type (I've enclosed copies of the new Pocket Pal and highlighted the parts I think you should use for your explanation)
Intro
First Generation (briefly mentioned)
Second Generation (the drawing and my caption explain it for me Do you want to do it this way or in Paragraphs)
Third Generation (basically the parts I have highlighted)
Then I thought we could mention some things are are important but not in direct line with the rest of the text. ie:
video display terminals VDTs
electronic editing
front end systems
word processing
CAM (composition and makeup systems
Personal computors
Galleys

I'll get to work on the next chapter right now.

Kind regards,

grandits

225 PARK AVENUE SOUTH, NEW YORK, NEW YORK 10003 • 212 254-1600 • TELEX 427195

Letter from an editor to an author

author can communicate directly through the keyboard. There are instances of authors and editors, many miles apart, working on the same manuscript at the same time—editing, rewriting, and correcting that manuscript by computer.

No matter in what form the work is submitted, in the course of this first reading editors will be watching for general organization, for improvements that might be achieved by reorganization of the manuscript. This could mean a rearrangement of chapters, or the lengthening or tightening of certain sections. In a novel, it could mean the further development of certain characters or even the elimination of some others; it might mean clarifying the motivations that lead to certain acts. In a biography, the editor could suggest additional material about a certain phase of the subject's life or a certain period in it. All of these imply relatively major changes and, as a result, serious discussions and exchanges of ideas with the author. Good editors never try to dictate; they suggest, as

108 4

printing areas. A water-receptive material that attaches itself only to the uncoated metal is then applied. In this way, the plate is divided into printing and nonprinting parts. This is a relatively inexpensive plate. The main disadvantage is environmental. Many harsh chemicals are needed and disposing of them becomes a problem.

The second type of offset plate, used for longer runs and able to produce a higher quality of printing, is called deep-etch. In these plates, the greasy printing areas are very slightly below the nonprinting ares, because the light-hardened coating has been removed and chemically made ink receptive in contrast to the wet non-printing areas. These plates differ, too, in that they are made with film positives rather than negatives.

The third kind of offset plate is called bimetal. Based on the principle of a light-sensitive protecting coating on a metal ink-receptive base, these plates are seldom used.

Once the plates have been made, actual printing can begin. Printing presses are complicated machines that must perform several functions. They must be capable of holding the plate firmly in position. They must be able to provide for the application of the ink essential to printing. Each press, too, must have

The "wave of the future" may be subtractive plates. All the chemicals are already on the plate when the printer buys them. After they are exposed to light they are developed in water. There is relatively no chemical residue. Very environmentally safe. They run longer. Unfortunately, right now, they are five times more expensive.

A manuscript page, with an editor's comments

persuasively but as tactfully as possible, for authors are, with good reason, sensitive about their work.

Once these major changes have been discussed, the editor should read the manuscript a second time for more specific suggestions. Editors look for factual errors, for unclear sentences, phrases that seem trite or overused. They make certain that authors have really said what they wanted to, and catch inconsistency in logic or characterization. If editors do not overextend their roles, and respect the individuality of the author, the latter will be more than grateful for any corrections or suggestions. Even the most careful author might say on one page that a character has blue eyes and on a later page that she has brown eyes; a sofa might be described as green on one page and as red on another. An author might well believe, too, that a point has been made, only to find that by following an editor's suggestion it might be made more clearly.

Depending on the specific nature of the book, the editors have further responsibilities. If there are to be photographs, they must see to it that they are placed properly in the text and that precise and accurate captions have been provided for them. If the book is a picture book for children, the editor will devote a great deal of time to the illustrator, making sure that the illustrations complement and extend the story.

An editor's job can be an immensely satisfying one, to which a good editor brings a broad cultural background, a knowledge of literature, and, above all, a love of books. By the time the editor and author (and illustrator, in some cases) have finished working together, most editorial problems should have been solved.

There does, however, remain one job: the preparation of the front and back matter—that is, the pages that come before the actual beginning of the text and after the end of that text.

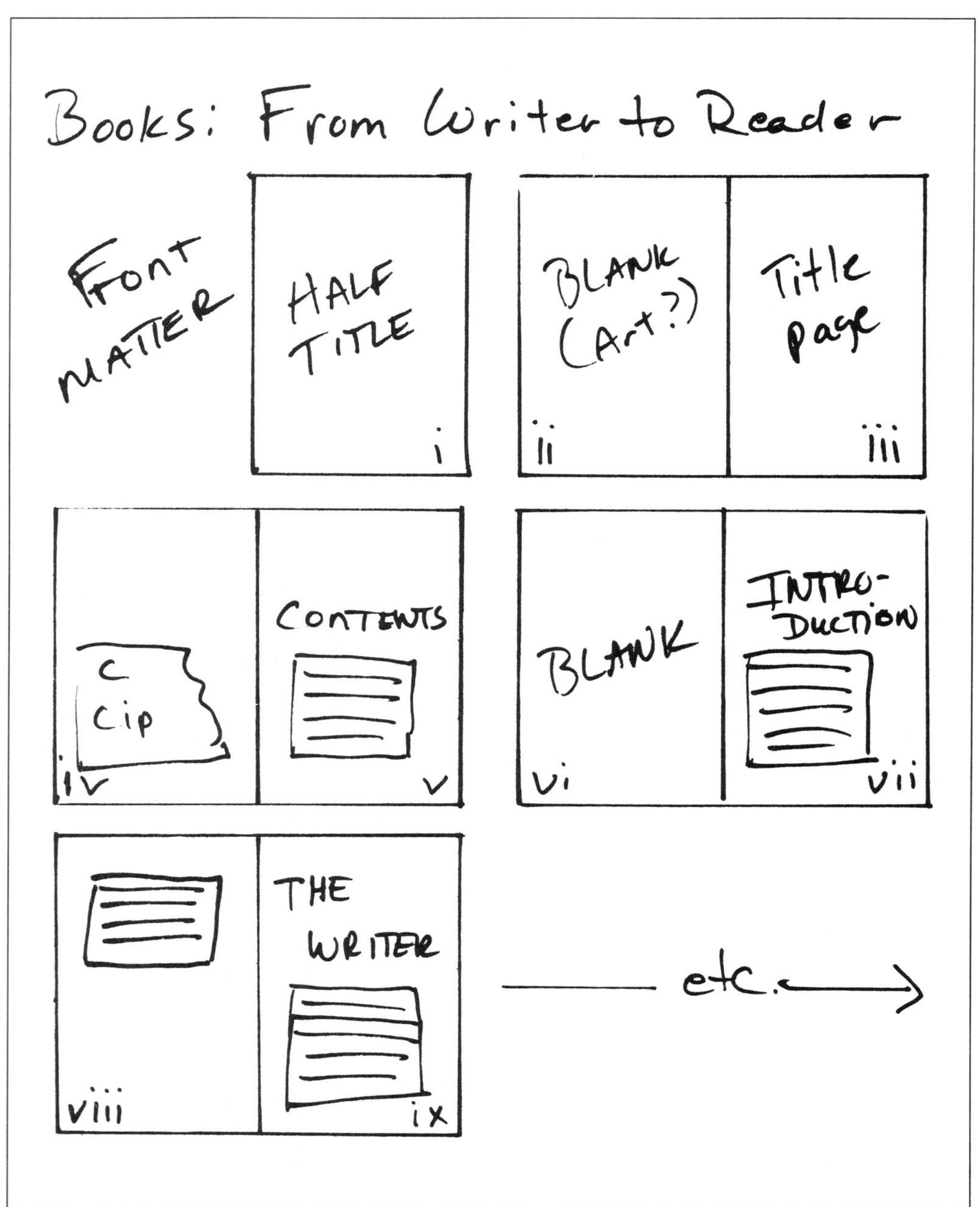

Thumbnail, showing editor's pagination of the front matter

These pages serve to give us more information about the book. The very first page will usually carry the name of the book, and it is usually called the half title, or the bastard. The next page might be blank, it might have a map or illustration, or it might be a card page and list the author's previously published books. The title page is third; it contains the title of the book as well as the name of the author, that of the publisher, and sometimes the date and place of publication. The fourth page is the copyright page, the page on which a copyright notice (the legal claim that the author or publisher, usually the former, makes to the work) is placed, as well as the Library of Congress Cataloging-in-Publication data, and, often, printing information. The following page has the dedication, if the volume is dedicated to someone, and this is followed by a table of contents. If there are illustrations in the book, a list of illustrations will sometimes follow. After that will come a foreword, preface, acknowledgments, and an introduction, if any or all of these are to be included in the book. (Sometimes, this order varies.) After these introductory pages, another half title is placed (this will be a part title if the book is divided into parts). That will be on a right-hand page; the reverse side is almost always blank and is generally followed by the beginning of the text itself. If all of these introductory pages are not ready by the time the manuscript leaves the editorial department—and this often happens—the fact that they are to come must be noted as an aid to the designer.

The same is true for the back matter, which follows the text. This will include appendixes and notes, supplementary material that will aid in understanding the text itself; a glossary, or definitions of various special terms used in the book; a bibliography, a list of books or articles used in researching the book, as well as of books that will be useful for further reading on the subject; and an index. The latter, of course, cannot be compiled until the book has actually been divided into pages.

The front and the back matter having been completed, the manuscript should be almost ready to be turned into a book. But before its initial stages of production and design, this manuscript must be carefully worked on by another kind of editor, called a copy editor. That job will be discussed in a later chapter.

(There is one notable exception to this rule, and that is the picture book for very young children, in which the role of the illustrator is equal in importance to that of the author of the text; the role of the illustrator will be fully dealt with in the following chapter.)

Before the manuscript is turned over to the copy editor, a manuscript transmittal form is prepared by the editor, and a copy of this form is sent not only to the copy editor but to the designer and to the production department as well. This form

Transmittal form

To:	J Schwartz	DA	JG	DA	MW	JG	Sharie	John G.		
From:	MW	JS	DA	[illegible]	JS	BR/MW	JS	JW		
Date:	7/5	7/6			8/16	8/16/88	8/18	9/21		
Due Date:	7/19							9/22		

Title: Before the Wild Flowers Bloom
Herewith: gg 1–27
Price:
Printing:

Backup: ms i–vi, 1–57.

To Come

This material is OK with no further corrections
Please initial:
Date:

WRITE COMMENTS AND INSTRUCTIONS HERE

One set of galleys needs to be returned keyed for artwork so dummy can be planned.

David— Please send 1 set for author review. Please key in art in 2nd set + return. Jean 7/5

Sent to author 7/6 — given to John 7/6

FM- 10
Text 1—70

Corrected gg JS 8/16

Sharie, please fix widows and discuss w/ me. John

is a summary of all the information on hand, and will be used as a guide throughout the various stages of the book's production.

Included on the form are the title of the book, the names of the author and the editor, the number of pages wanted, the number of books to be printed, the trim size, and the tentative price. In addition, there are the names of the designer and the production supervisor, the date on which finished books are wanted, and the proposed date of publication.

The editor provides, too, every possible detail concerning the manuscript. This includes a list of what makes up the front matter and what makes up the back matter—noting what material is already on hand and what is to come. There is a list of special matter to be included that is not part of the text: illustrations, frontispiece, endpapers, captions, graphs, charts, and so on. A note has to be made of the extent of any special matter in the text, as well as a list of chapter and part titles, main heads, subheads, subsubheads, and the precise nature and importance of these. Mention must be made of running heads, those single lines on the tops of pages which run throughout the book as an aid to the reader.

Proof requirements, too, are noted on this form: just how many sets of proofs are required, and approximately how much time will be needed to read them. Finally, there must be information about the jacket—the artwork as well as the written material—and about exactly what must be printed on the book's jacket.

When the editor has summarized all this information, the manuscript is ready to be copyedited; after that, it will be designed and put into production. A great deal has been done, but the job of making a book is a little less than half completed.

THE ILLUSTRATOR

Just as writers express themselves through words, illustrators express themselves by means of pictures. Illustrations are often used in textbooks, technical books, how-to books, and lavish gift editions, or coffee table books. They are frequently required for book jackets, and illustrated novels or stories, once very popular, are regaining some of that popularity today. Yet we most commonly associate illustrated books with children's books, and references to illustrators in this chapter generally mean illustrators of books for young readers—although all illustrators go through similar steps.

Illustrators, like writers, are individuals, and no one illustrator is exactly like another. They all work in different ways and in different styles, often utilizing different methods. They are creative artists, and they depend upon inspiration, which can be drawn not only from the text to be illustrated but also from many other sources and personal experiences.

Unlike writers, however, in most cases illustrators need

special training to pursue their careers. Techniques and craftsmanship must be learned, either through years of full-time study at an art school or at least through a course of part-time studies. Illustrators must have an expert knowledge of drawing and of the various mediums of artistic expression. An understanding of the history of art and of the various schools of art and design is also important. Important, too, is a thorough familiarity with printing, so that the illustrator may best know how to prepare the artwork for the printer. Above all, however, the illustrator is an artist, who must have a good eye and a vivid imagination.

The problems that an illustrator faces in finding a publisher are somewhat different from those that face a writer. The reason for this is obvious: the illustrator must have something to illustrate, and unless he has illustrated his own story, which is occasionally the case, it is the editor or art director who will ask to have illustrations prepared for a text written by someone else. Because of this, it is essential that inexperienced illustrators carefully prepare portfolios of their work which can be shown to prospective publishers.

Hudson Talbott, an illustrator, at work

It is impossible to overemphasize the importance of this portfolio, usually the only instrument which enables an illustrator to find work. Its purpose is to demonstrate the range of style, versatility, and professionalism of the illustrator's skills. It aims to show that the person looking for work is able to illustrate a children's book, and not necessarily that he or she is a "great" artist—abstract art, no matter how good, would most likely be out of place in the portfolio. In addition to presenting evidence of the illustrator's artistic strengths and individuality, the portfolio should make clear the illustrator's knowledge of printing techniques, of what can and cannot be done.

Each portfolio, of course, will be different—the work of an individual artist—but every portfolio must include representative examples of the illustrator's work in color and in black and white, and in as many styles as possible. As subject matter, drawings of children or animals are especially appropriate, since they are often the subjects of children's books. (Extra copies of some of these samples should be prepared as well, so that a copy of one or more drawings can be left behind in a publisher's office as a reminder of the illustrator's work.) A small dummy layout of an illustrated story—a folk tale or a fairy tale, or possibly one written by the artist—could be most helpful in showing the illustrator's ability to draw in sequence, to pace a story, and to develop and maintain a character. Included, too, in this portfolio would be any samples of the illustrator's previously published work as well as a concise biographical résumé of his or her education and experience in the field.

Once this portfolio has been neatly and professionally prepared, the illustrator is ready to look for a publisher. There are many publishers of children's books, and the illustrator

SIX STYLES OF ILLUSTRATION

Watercolor (Teryl Euvremer)

Pen and ink (Jill Bennett)

Marker (Marvin Glass)

As for me, at the victory parade
I was appointed Postmaster General.

Cut paper (Edward Miller)

Linoleum cut (Gail E. Haley)

Brush and ink (June Gaddy)

can determine which house would be best suited for his or her work in a number of ways. Visits to libraries and bookstores will give a good idea of which publishers publish what kinds of books. A careful perusal of children's book catalogues, too, will be most helpful. Addresses and telephone numbers of publishers can be found in *Literary Market Place, Writer's Market,* and *Artist's Market,* as can the names of people in each firm to be contacted. Further and more detailed information can be obtained from the Children's Book Council.

When it has been determined which publishers seem most likely to be interested in the illustrator's work, appointments should, if possible, be made with the appropriate members of the publishing houses. (Some houses prefer to see sample illustrations before granting personal appointments.) Whether the person to be seen is the children's book editor or the art director depends on the structure of the house, but in most cases the editor will be more useful, for the editor knows first what books are scheduled for future publication.

This meeting is, of course, of great importance. Chance plays a part. It is possible that the artist might walk into the editor's office during a period when that editor is looking for someone to illustrate a manuscript that is particularly suited to that artist's style. This might lead to an immediate assignment, but such a coincidence is most unlikely. It is far more probable that in the course of that meeting the editor will merely have a first opportunity to get acquainted with the illustrator's work, by examining the portfolio and discussing its contents with the artist. At the conclusion of the meeting, the editor will file the artist's name for future possible use, making note of his or her special skills and talents and filing as well samples of the illustrator's work.

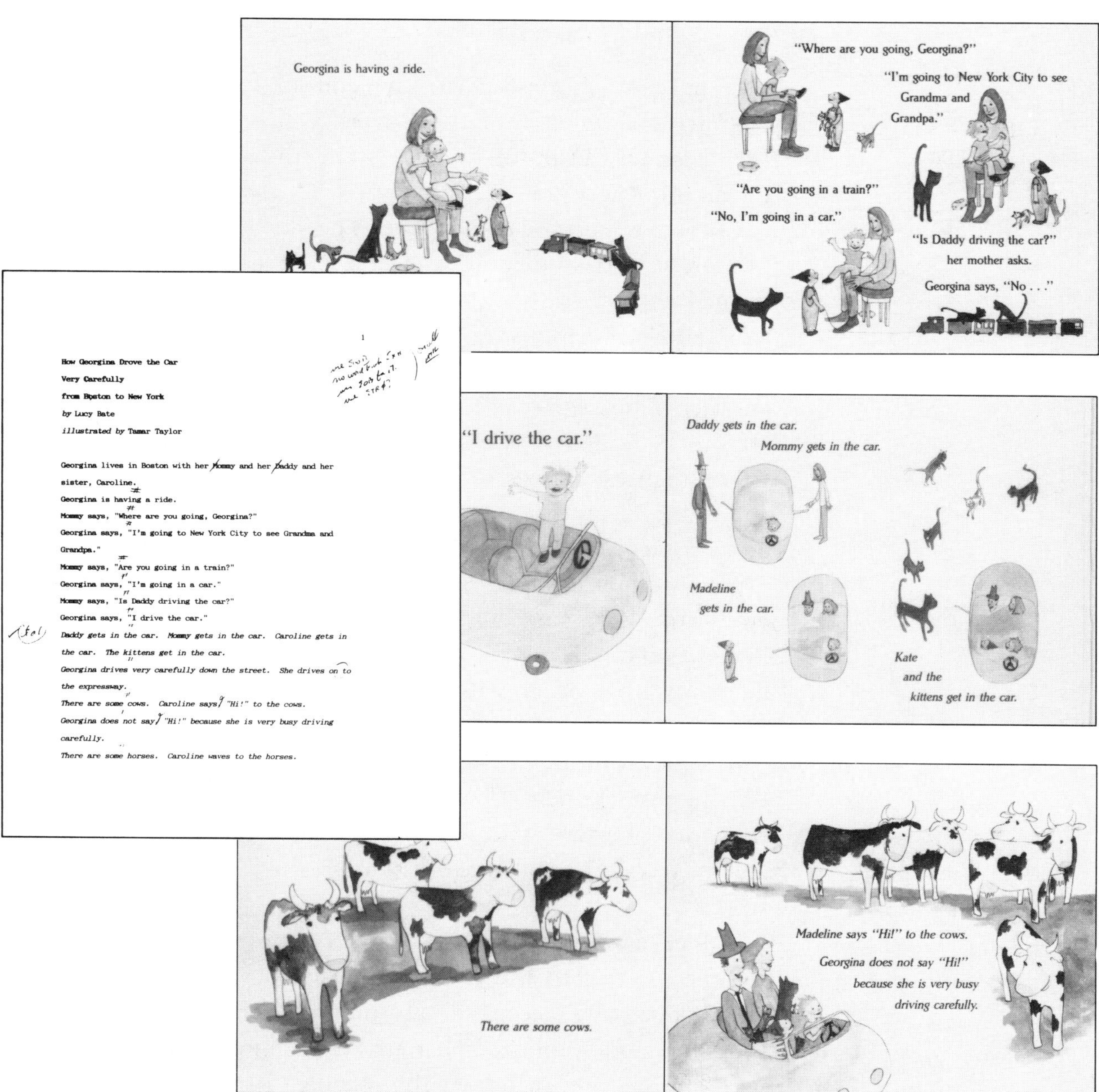

1

How Georgina Drove the Car
Very Carefully
from Boston to New York
by Lucy Bate
illustrated by Tamar Taylor

Georgina lives in Boston with her Mommy and her Daddy and her sister, Caroline.

Georgina is having a ride.

Mommy says, "Where are you going, Georgina?"

Georgina says, "I'm going to New York City to see Grandma and Grandpa."

Mommy says, "Are you going in a train?"

Georgina says, "I'm going in a car."

Mommy says, "Is Daddy driving the car?"

Georgina says, "I drive the car."

Daddy gets in the car. Mommy gets in the car. Caroline gets in the car. The kittens get in the car.

Georgina drives very carefully down the street. She drives on to the expressway.

There are some cows. Caroline says, "Hi!" to the cows.

Georgina does not say, "Hi!" because she is very busy driving carefully.

There are some horses. Caroline waves to the horses.

Tamar Taylor's illustrations add to Lucy Bate's text for How Georgina Drove the Car Very Carefully from Boston to New York

The next step is up to the editor, who must decide whether and when the artist's work will be used, and it is useful for an illustrator to understand the steps involved in making this decision.

It begins with the manuscript to be illustrated. Once it has been read and studied by the editor, that editor will have formed an idea of the kind of art that will be required. The story might be funny or serious, modern or traditional; it might call for bright colors or soft colors, for one technique or another. Thus, the editor will have a basic idea of the kind of art the story demands before looking for an illustrator. The field is highly competitive. There are inexperienced illustrators to be considered—talented artists who have left information and samples of their work at publishing houses—and there are experienced illustrators, eager to find new work, to be considered. Most experienced illustrators work for several publishing houses and can do two or more books a year; no publisher can guarantee that there will be enough books suited to one artist's style over a given period of time.

Because of this, editors have a wide choice; they must not only be aware of new talent, but must also be acquainted with the work of artists who have already been published and be able to recognize that one illustrator's style would fit a given story.

Once a decision has been made, the editor will then submit the text to the potential illustrator, who will decide whether or not to accept the assignment. If the illustrator likes the story and wants to illustrate it, preliminary discussions with the editor will follow the reading. If the artist is well established and is extensively published, no samples will be necessary. If, on the other hand, the artist is less well known, he or she will most likely be asked to prepare sample illustrations before going ahead with the contract. In fairness to the artist, no editor should ever ask more than one illustrator to sample the same story at the same time.

If the sample is acceptable, an agreement can be drawn up; if it is nearly acceptable, more discussion and revision will be required. If, however, the sample seems hopeless, the editor is forced to reject it and look for another illustrator. In order to avoid disappointments of this kind, much thought and consideration must be given before an illustrator is asked to prepare a sample.

Once the contract has been drawn up—and its terms generally reflect the relationship of the illustrations to the text as well as the experience of the artist—the actual work can begin. For the artist, it is challenging and often exhilarating work, a creative experience equal to that enjoyed by the author of the text.

It is the editor, and not the author, with whom the illustrator will work, for it is the editor who will most likely encourage the artist's own creativity. The editor will at this point discuss with the illustrator the trim size of the book and the number of pages wanted, as well as the number of colors that will be used. In addition, they will discuss the pacing of the book and the balance between illustrations and text. Illustrations require movement and vitality in the same way that text does; they must be carefully paced and must reflect the tensions and climaxes of the text itself. Ideally, the illustrations should be able to stand on their own, to tell the story even without the accompanying text.

The illustrator's first job is to prepare small, rough thumbnail sketches of the entire book. This will enable the illustrator to plan where pictures will fall, the pacing of the story, and the color and composition themes. The sketches are brought to

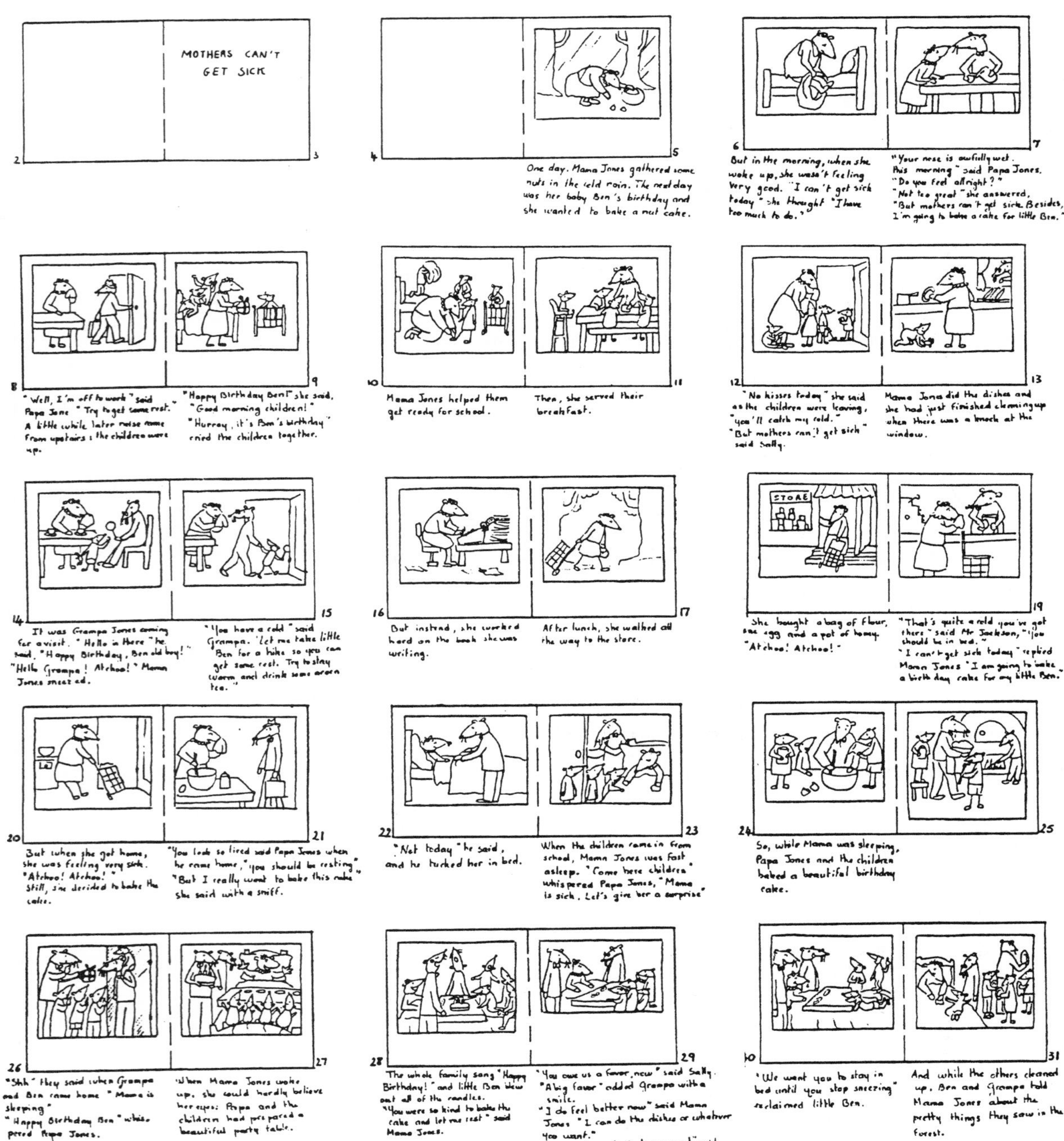

Book thumbnail for Mothers Can't Get Sick *written and illustrated by Sylvie Wickstrom*

the editor and discussed. After these discussions, the artist prepares a rough, full-size dummy, generally in black and white. In some cases, the artist takes a copy of the manuscript (if the type is not yet set), cuts it up, and lays it out on the pages. In other cases, the editor or art director will give the artist blank dummy pages with a copy of the text broken up and pasted in it. Sketches of the illustrations are then made in relation to the text.

This initial rough dummy is brought to the editor who studies it carefully, often conferring with the art director and other members of the department. The artist is then called in, and there is further discussion. If the suggested revisions are minor, the artist will take back this black-and-white dummy and begin to prepare a rough color dummy; if there are to be extensive revisions, a second rough black-and-white dummy will have to be made before work on the color dummy can proceed.

The procedure for the rough color dummy is essentially the same as that for the previous dummy. Preparation on the part of the artist, this time using color, is followed by discussion, this time more detailed, with the editor or art director. Technical aspects, the use of color, and budgetary restrictions are clarified. It must be remembered, incidentally, that since not all books for children are works of fantasy, a great deal of research may be required by the illustrator, who could be called upon to represent pictorially many periods in history and many places. Studies of costumes of various times or countries, of furnishings, and of landscapes could be essential, and the illustrator might have to spend many hours poring through libraries and museums, finding ideas, and learning details essential to the accurate rendering of the work.

Once the rough color dummy has been accepted, the artist

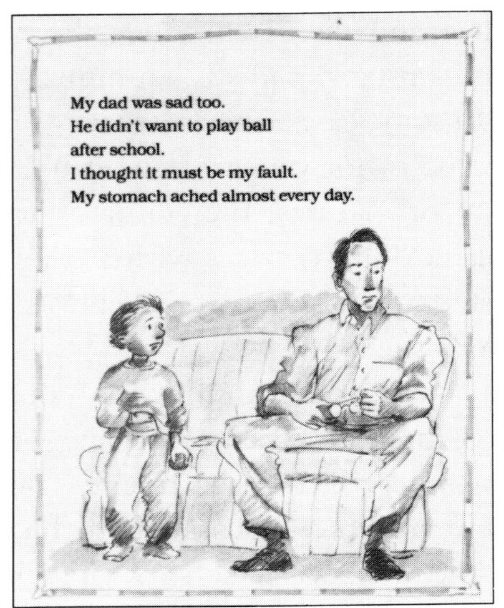

SKETCH AND FINISH
Cat Bowman Smith, Sometimes a Family Has to Split Up *(top)*
Jack Ziegler, Flying Boy *(bottom)*

prepares the final artwork with the aid of a layout provided by the production department. This layout gives the exact dimensions of the inside of the book and of the jacket. Color work is prepared in one of two ways: it is either camera-separated by the printer, or it is preseparated by the illustrator. In the former case, the artist prepares the illustrations in color as a painter would, using one of many ways of expression. Different illustrators are more comfortable in different mediums, and some books call for one medium while others would best be executed in other ways. Pen and ink, watercolor, collage, oil, pencil and oil glazes, gouache, and tempera are among the many mediums used by book illustrators. These illustrations are then turned over to the printer, whose job—including camera separation—will be discussed in the chapter on the color printer.

Occasionally illustrators are asked to preseparate their art themselves. Separating colors means preparing the art with separate black-and-white copy for each color to be used. The illustrator, of course, will have been told how many colors can be allowed by the budget, and will have to work within those

Preseparated art by Giulio Maestro for the book Dollars and Cents for Harriet

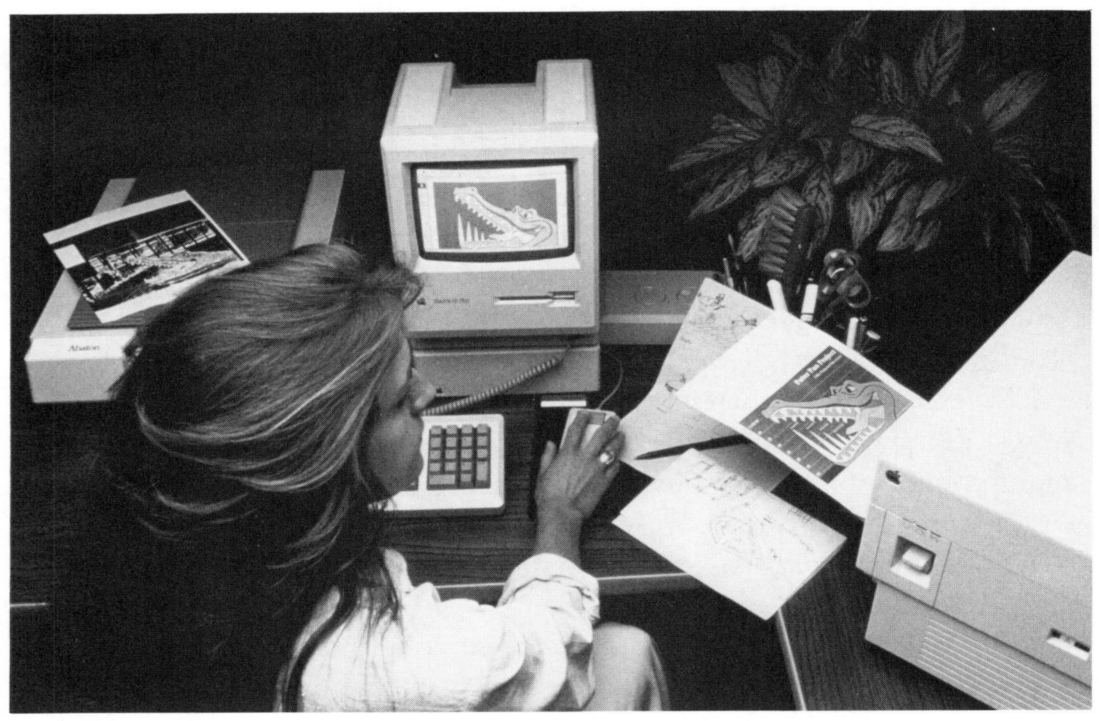

Art done on a computer

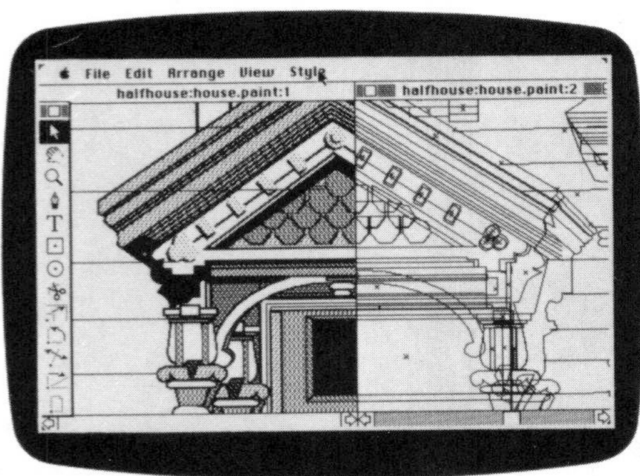

limitations. If four colors are allowed, the artist can obtain a vast number of color tints by combining the four basic colors: black, yellow, blue, and red. If three colors are allowed, there will be fewer possible tints, and there will obviously be even fewer if only two colors can be used.

Once the colors have been chosen from a color guide published by an ink company, the illustrator prepares the art for each page of the book. The parts that are to be printed in the most important color—usually black—are placed on a board, or a sheet of special white cardboard. This is called the key plate and it contains the line drawing or outline for the illustration, which gives it definition. The areas for other colors are presented on transparent acetate or watercolor-paper overlays that are taped on top of the board. (Watercolor paper is used if a wash effect is wanted.)

The color is indicated on each overlay. For example, the illustrator, after having prepared the black key plate, will mount a piece of acetate with masking tape for the blue plate and proceed to paint (in black) all those areas that should be printed in blue. Once done, the same procedure will be used for the red plate and then for the yellow plate. The overlays for each color plate show only blobs of black—there are no lines—but these blobs show a variation in density. This is because the illustrator has indicated and can obtain light and dark variations of each color he wants, which will determine the density of the color. There are ways of mixing percentages of colors that will combine to bring about entirely different colors. Tubes of paint which the illustrator may purchase are marked by screen percentages (50%, 25%, 10%, etc.) and the results of the many combinations can be foreseen by the illustrator with the use of color charts.

Another important job for the illustrator in the preparation of the art is to make certain that the register is exact—that is, to see that each overlay is in correct position relative to the key plate and the other overlays. This is achieved by putting register marks on the key plate and on each subsequent overlay and making certain that they align perfectly. Since acetate is transparent, it presents no problem for the illustrator, but when using watercolor paper, the illustrator must mount the overlays over the glass top of a light box, which is illuminated by lights that shine from the bottom.

Before turning in the artwork, the illustrator must carefully check the register as well as the consistency in the density of ink on each page. If, for example, there is a green shirt that recurs throughout the book, it is essential that this green shirt have the same amount of ink on each of the plates showing that shirt.

In recent years, the computer has become a valuable tool for technical illustrations. Today, illustrators or authors can make their own graphs, charts, and blueprint-style drawings on a home computer with excellent results. Changes are easy to make, and they can even be done in color. When these illustrations are printed out on a laser printer, the results can be as sharp and accurate as well-rendered mechanical drawings. In the near future, it will be possible to make fine illustrations with the use of a color computer.

The illustrator's job is one that calls for technical skills as well as creative ones. Illustrators will even be called upon and will want to check their work when the book is on press. It is also a rewarding job: to express through images what a writer has expressed through words, and to see that the writer's intentions have been faithfully carried out.

THE COPY EDITOR

The reader is never aware of a copy editor's work if the job is done well, but very much aware of it if it has been done improperly. For this reason, copy editors seldom receive the credit they deserve. Theirs is an essential job, a complex and difficult one, requiring intelligence, precision, and care.

Copy editors are the last people in the editorial department to read a manuscript carefully. It is their responsibility to check the manuscript for accuracy—in many cases finding errors that the authors and editors have overlooked—and to "style" the manuscript. In this case, style does not refer to literary style, but rather spelling, consistency, and usage. The copy editor's most useful tools (in addition to an eye for spelling) are a good, comprehensive dictionary and one of several handbooks of style such as *Words into Type,* the University of Chicago Press's *The Chicago Manual of Style,* or *Chicago Guide to Preparing Electronic Manuscripts,* all of them valuable guides to correct usage. If a manuscript is prepared on a computer or word processor, a copy editor must check the author's disk. In addition, some publishing houses have their own "house" style, a guide to usage preferred by that one house, usually issued to the copy editors and sometimes to authors who are writing for that house.

The problems that a copy editor encounters are innumerable and often unexpected, for each manuscript is different. Consistency is of fundamental importance, and this entails a great deal of checking back and forth in the manuscript. A few examples of this will best illustrate the scope of the copy editor's job.

Consistent spelling is one example; many words can be spelled more than one way, neither being necessarily right or wrong, and the spelling of each word should be the same throughout the book. Should it be wristwatch or wrist watch, postoperative or post-operative? Capitalization too should be

The Chicago Manual of Style

The 13th Edition of A Manual of Style Revised and Expanded

The Chicago Manual of Style *and pages from* Words into Type

DASH

5.82 There are several kinds of dashes, differing from one another according to length. There are en dashes, em dashes, and 2- and 3-em dashes. Each kind of dash has its own uses. The most commonly used dash is the em dash. In the following material, the em dash is referred to simply as "the dash." The other dashes are identified.

SUDDEN BREAKS AND ABRUPT CHANGES

5.83 A dash or a pair of dashes is used to denote a sudden break in thought that causes an abrupt change in sentence structure (see also 5.12, 5.38, 5.97–99):

> "Will he—can he—obtain the necessary signatures?" Mills said pointedly.
>
> The Platonic world of the static and the Hegelian world of process—how great the contrast!
>
> Consensus—that was the will-o'-the-wisp he doggedly pursued.
>
> The chancellor—he had been awake half the night waiting in vain for a reply—came down to breakfast in an angry mood.
>
> There came a time—let us say, for convenience, with Herodotus and Thucydides—when this attention to actions was conscious and deliberate.

An entry from The Chicago Manual of Style

consistent, and with the aid of a dictionary and stylebook, the copy editor must decide when to use Prime Minister and when to use prime minister, Eighteenth Century or eighteenth century, the General or the general. Dates must be written the same way throughout—November 18, 1975, or 18 November 1975—and a decision must be made whether to represent numbers by figures (32) or by words (thirty-two). The copy editor must make certain that the titles of books will be set in italics—*The Great Gatsby,* for example—and that titles of short stories ("The Rich Boy") will be set in roman type within quotation marks.

The above are merely a few examples of consistency that a copy editor must watch for. Other responsibilities include verifying names, dates, and places—any facts that might have escaped the attention of the author and editor. In some cases,

39 Colorado/Bylinsky

Frank was quiet.

A fast knock on the door startled us. Danny, Aunt Peppina's oldest son, stood in the doorway. His shoes were layered with mud. His gloves were worn thin. As he unbuttoned his coat, a red scarf peeked out, halfway hidden below his chin. His watersoaked feet sloshed on the scrubbed floor. Mama would be angry if she saw the muddy footprints.

Frank and Danny were both the same age, thirteen. Danny sat down on Frank's bed.

"Eveyone is waiting at the machine shop near the entrance of the mine. The rescue workers just finished their shift, but there's no news yet," he said.

Mama and Aunt Peppina were waiting there with all the other women. Mama didn't want us to leave the house and she sure didn't want any of us down by the machine shop.

Danny whispered into Frank's ear. He jumped out of the bed and pulled on his clothes.

"Mama will be mad if she finds out you left the house," I said.

"She won't find out because no one's going to tell on me, Carm. We're just going for a walk, I don't know when we'll be back."

They both left. Danny's wet footsteps followed him across the room. The dark grey ovals floated on top of the grey floor. I watched the footsteps until the floor soaked

A copy-edited manuscript

obviously, an author's expertise has to be taken for granted, and this kind of fact-checking should be unnecessary. In others—and the editor of the book should indicate this to the copy editor—it is wise for the latter to double-check.

In addition to making sure that the style is consistent throughout the manuscript and to the checking of facts, the copy editor's job is that of preparing the manuscript for the designer and compositor. For the compositor, or typesetter, the copy editor prepares the manuscript in such a way that everything is legible and correct, so the manuscript can be accurately set. For the designer, the copy editor should indicate all matter that is not straight text, that will have to be designed differently. It is the copy editor's job to point out matter such as chapter headings and subchapter headings. It is important to call the designer's attention to poetry or extracts, words that should be set off in a manner different from that of the main body of the text. Footnotes must be checked to see

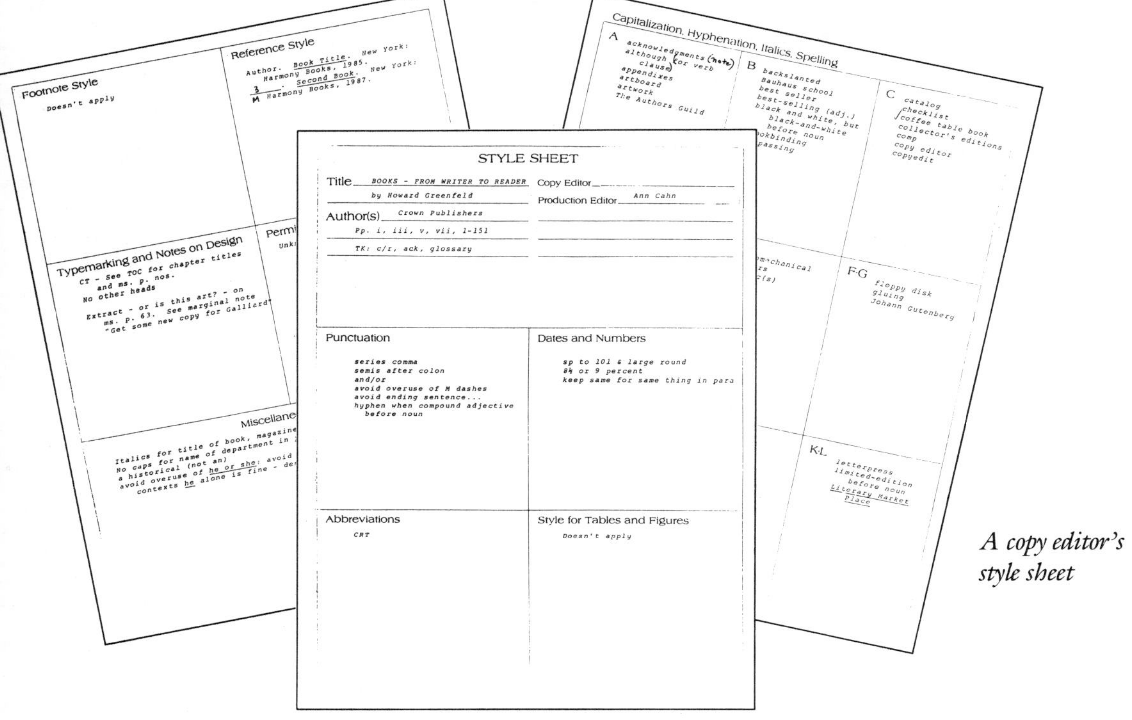

STYLE SHEET

Title BOOKS - FROM WRITER TO READER
by Howard Greenfeld
Author(s) Crown Publishers
Pp. i, iii, v, vii, 1-151
TK: c/r, ack, glossary

Copy Editor
Production Editor Ann Cahn

Punctuation

series comma
semis after colon
and/or
avoid overuse of M dashes
avoid ending sentence...
hyphen when compound adjective before noun

Dates and Numbers

sp to 101 & large round
8½ or 9 percent
keep same for same thing in para

Abbreviations

CRT

Style for Tables and Figures

Doesn't apply

A copy editor's style sheet

that they are properly placed, and the chapter titles in the table of contents should, of course, correspond to the order and exact name in which they are found in the text. Although this might seem obvious, all too often mistakes are made in this seemingly simple step in the making of a book. It is better to check each detail too carefully than not carefully enough, for corrections that have to be made later in proofs are costly.

The copy editor must prepare a style sheet, reflecting all the decisions that were made in styling the manuscript editorially. Sometimes a list of characters and/or of place names may be required as well. The copy editor may also be asked to keep a list of any items, such as lines of poetry or of popular songs, for which permission to reprint will be necessary.

Most publishing houses today do not have in-house copy editors. Production editors, who traffic each stage of a book, are in charge of freelancing the copyediting and proofreading work. They check the quality of the freelancer's job and work closely with the editor, designer, and production supervisor to make sure that the final book is of the highest quality.

Once the manuscript has been copyedited, it is ready to leave the editorial department. Before it is designed and actually set into type, one precaution might be called for: When there is any possible question of libel, it is essential to have the manuscript read by a lawyer if this has not already been done.

THE DESIGNER

Before a manuscript can be turned into a book, it must be designed. By this we mean that specifications must be given as to how the book should look physically. The alternatives are many, for books differ widely not only in editorial content but also in appearance.

Basically, the book designer's job is to carry out visually what the author has done with words. In order to conceive these visual aspects, the designer must call upon a wide variety of skills. His or her background usually includes study in an art school. A knowledge of the various movements that make up the history of art and industrial design—such as neoclassicism, Victorian design, or the Bauhaus school—can influence the choice of a design, and the designer often finds inspiration in the work of predecessors. The designer must have a sense of color, form, space, and texture as well as a thorough knowledge of printing and book production, so as to know what is and what is not possible. Since with modern technology almost anything is possible, the designer must be very much aware of the economic consequences of any decision taken—whether that decision is within the limits of the budget set for a given book. Above all, a designer must realize the function and limits of good book design. The design might enhance the text, but if it is obtrusive, if it calls too much attention to itself as design, then the book has not been successfully designed.

Before beginning work, a designer must understand thoroughly the nature of the manuscript to be designed. At the time that a particular job is assigned, there will most likely be a preliminary discussion with the editor. Essential information, too, will be given by the production supervisor. At this stage decisions are made concerning trim size, length of the book, binding, and the general feel of the book.

A careful reading of the manuscript follows. The designer becomes familiar with its style, the feeling it generates, and the market for which it is being published. During this reading, ideas for design and for possible typefaces will be noted as will any special problems that may be involved. These latter will concern chapter headings, subheads, and notes, and where it would be best to place those notes—at the bottom of the page as footnotes, at the end of each chapter, or at the very end of the entire text.

While interpreting the manuscript accurately, the designer must also keep in mind that the finished book must be attractive and able to be read as comfortably and pleasurably as possible. When this reading is finished, there is sometimes another discussion with the editor and/or the production supervisor. After this, the designer should have a full understanding of the problems and challenges to be met.

The designer's first important decision concerns the selection of a typeface. In order to make this choice, it is necessary to know which compositor will be setting the book and then

Caslon Old Face #2 *Van Dijck* *Jenson*

g g g

Fairfield *Cheltenham* *Baskerville #2*

g g g

Century Old Style *Calvert* *Futura*

g g g

EXAMPLES OF LOWERCASE G'S

to study the prospective compositor's specimen books to know what is available. To most readers, it might seem that all the letters that make up the words of all books are the same: a g is always a g. In a sense, this is correct since almost all words are printed in what we call roman letters or italic letters. However, upon close examination of several books, it will become clear that there are a tremendous number of different styles of type, developed over the centuries, within the overall classification of roman and italic. Type design is a complicated and painstaking art that involves not only considerations of esthetic beauty, but also a careful study of the combination and compatibility of an alphabet of letters as well as of numbers and punctuation marks. Many typefaces, such as Caslon and Baskerville, are named after their creators.

The differences among the many kinds of typefaces can be noted by carefully examining each letter; what may seem to be the same is often not. A letter is made up of various parts. Some have an upper stroke, called the ascender (as in *d*), and some have a downward stroke, called the descender (as in *y*); there is sometimes a smaller line that finishes off a main stroke of a letter, which is called a serif; and each letter has what is called a main body. The differences in the strokes, the serifs, and the main body are the factors that distinguish one typeface from another. Some letters have strokes of comparatively uniform thickness, while others show extreme contrast between thick and thin strokes. The letters of some typefaces have no serifs at all, and the letters of others have either rounded serifs or pointed or square serifs.

Typefaces have been placed in several categories, and it is useful to mention them, although the distinctions are often very fine and there is a certain amount of overlapping among categories.

One category is designated as old style. Old-style typefaces

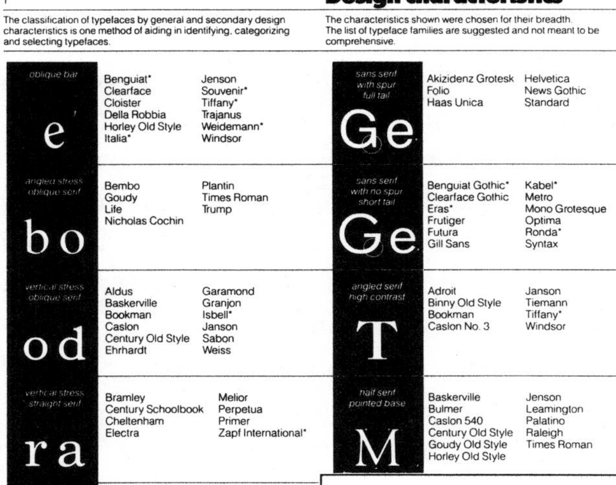

T

Design characteristics

The classification of typefaces by general and secondary design characteristics is one method of aiding in identifying, categorizing and selecting typefaces.

The characteristics shown were chosen for their breadth. The list of typeface families are suggested and not meant to be comprehensive.

oblique bar — e
Benguiat*, Clearface, Cloister, Della Robbia, Horley Old Style, Italia*, Jenson, Souvenir*, Tiffany*, Trajanus, Weidemann*, Windsor

angled stress oblique serif — bo
Bembo, Goudy, Life, Nicholas Cochin, Plantin, Times Roman, Trump

vertical stress oblique serif — od
Aldus, Baskerville, Bookman, Caslon, Century Old Style, Ehrhardt, Garamond, Granjon, Isbell*, Janson, Sabon, Weiss

vertical stress straight serif — ra
Bramley, Century Schoolbook, Cheltenham, Electra, Melior, Perpetua, Primer, Zapf International*

straight serif high contrast — nu
Auriga, Basilia Haas, Bodoni, Century, Fenice*, Pilgrim, Promoter, Tiemann, Torino, Walbaum

square serif — Lh
A&S Gallatin, Beton, City, Clarendon, Egyptian, Glypha, Lubalin Graph*, Memphis, Rockwell, Serifa, Stymie

half or hybrid serif — Ii
Americana, Barcelona*, Copperplate, Friz Quadrata*, Icone, Korinna*, Newtext*, Novarese*, Pegasus, Serif Gothic*

sans serif with spur full tail — Ge
Akizidenz Grotesk, Folio, Haas Unica, Helvetica, News Gothic, Standard

sans serif with no spur short tail — Ge
Benguiat Gothic*, Clearface Gothic, Eras*, Frutiger, Futura, Gill Sans, Kabel*, Metro, Mono Grotesque, Optima, Ronda*, Syntax

angled serif high contrast — T
Adroit, Binny Old Style, Bookman, Caslon No. 3, Janson, Tiemann, Tiffany*, Windsor

hair serif pointed base — M
Baskerville, Bulmer, Caslon 540, Century Old Style, Goudy Old Style, Horley Old Style, Jenson, Leamington, Palatino, Raleigh, Times Roman

Design characteristics and parts of a character

Parts of a Character

S

Arm
Horizontal stroke free on one end.

Bar
Horizontal stroke in the A,H,e,t, and similar letters.

Bowl
Curved stroke which makes an enclosed space within a character

Counter
The fully, or partially enclosed space within a character.

Ear
Small stroke projecting from the top of the lowercase g.

Loop
The lower portion of the lowercase roman g.

Serif
A line crossing the main strokes of a character.

Shoulder
Curved stroke of the h,m, and n.

Stem
A straight vertical stroke, or main straight diagonal stroke in a letter.

Descender
Part of the letters g,j,p,q,y, that extends below the baseline.

Ascender
Part of the lowercase letters that extends above the height of the lowercase.

Terminal
End of a stroke not terminated with a serif.

x-Height
The height of the lowercase letters.

Cap Height
The height of a capital letter.

Tail
Descender of Q or short diagonal stroke of the R.

Swash
Fancy flourish replacing a terminal or serif.

are characterized by open, wide, round letters, strokes of relatively uniform thickness, and rounded or pointed serifs. Examples of old style are Garamond, Caslon, and Janson.

The other major category is called modern (though not what we think of as modern, since it was designed over two hundred years ago). The letters in these typefaces are more mechanically perfect; there is great contrast between thick and thin strokes; the shading is heavy; and the serifs are thin and straight. Examples of modern typefaces include Times Roman, Caledonia, and Bodoni.

In between old style and modern are those typefaces that are called transitional. These are more angular than old style, with sharper contrast between thick and thin strokes. The most widely used of these typefaces is Baskerville.

Finally, there are square serif (or Egyptian) and sans serif (or Gothic). The former, of which Clarendon and Cairo are examples, have square serifs, uniform strokes, and little contrast; the latter, of which Helvetica, News Gothic, and Futura are examples, are perfectly plain, with no serifs and strokes of uniform thickness.

The differences in typefaces may be subtle, but the overall effect of the use of one typeface rather than another can be very important, and for this reason the choice of the right typeface for any given book is perhaps the designer's most difficult job. Depending on this choice, the book may have a feeling of lightness or heaviness, of informality or formality.

Once the designer has selected the typeface most suited to the manuscript, the next concern will be the size of the type. Type is measured in points, and generally is available in sizes from six points to seventy-two points. However, the most common type sizes for the main text of a book—because they are the most legible—are ten and eleven point. These will not

Caslon No. 540 *Old style*
abcdefghijklmnopqrstuvwxyz
ABCDEFGHIJKLMNOPQRSTUVWXYZ
1234567890 (&.,:;!?'""-*$¢%/)

Clarendon *Square serif*
abcdefghijklmnopqrstuvwxyz
ABCDEFGHIJKLMNOPQRSTUVWXYZ
1234567890(&.,:;!?''""-–—-·[]*$¢%/£)

Bauer Bodoni *Modern*
abcdefghijklmnopqrstuvwxyz
ABCDEFGHIJKLMNOPQRSTUVWXYZ
1234567890 (&.,:;!?'""-$/£)

Baskerville *Transitional*
abcdefghijklmnopqrstuvwxyz
ABCDEFGHIJKLMNOPQRSTUV
WXYZ 1234567890 (&.,:;!?'""-*$¢%/)

Helvetica *Sans serif*
abcdefghijklmnopqrstuvwxyz
ABCDEFGHIJKLMNOPQRSTUVWXYZ
1234567890 (&.,:;!?'""-*$¢%/£)

THE FIVE MAJOR TYPE STYLES

be used for books for young children, or books especially designed for elderly people who may have poor eyesight, both of whom would require larger type, but for the average reader they are the most acceptable sizes.

Type is also measured by width, but this measurement comes into account at the time the typeface is being chosen. The reason for this is that each single typeface is classified according to character per pica (designated as c.p.p.), which permits the designer to know how many characters of any typeface can fit on one line, depending, of course, on the length of that line. The designer's choice of a typeface, in that case, could be influenced not only by esthetic reasons, but by the publisher's desire to have a book that seems longer or shorter, whichever the case may be.

In addition to specifying the typeface and its size, as well as the length of the line, the designer must decide on the amount of space wanted between each line. This is called leading (pronounced LEDD-ing); it is measured in points and is determined by the size of the type to be used and the length of the line. The designer will sum up the requirements for the composition of the main text of a book, for example, by calling for "Baskerville 10/11 × 23." This means 10-point Baskerville, with 1 point of leading, and a line that measures 23 picas.

One area in which the designer has great freedom to assert

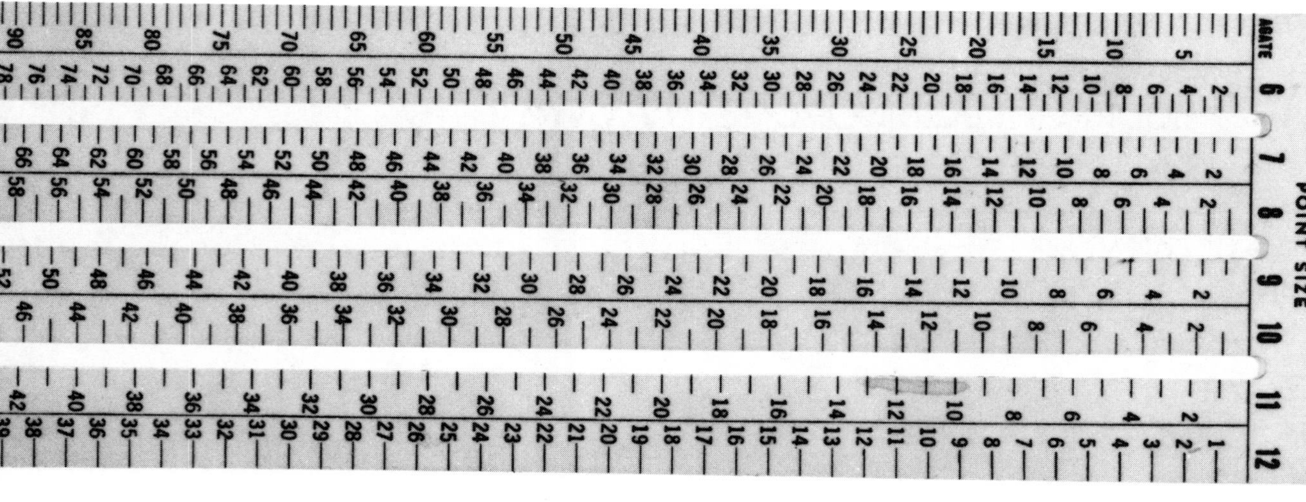

A type gauge

personal taste is in the design of the title page, part titles, and chapter openings. These often involve the use of what are called display faces—that is, type that is used to display, to call attention through a larger size.

There are a large number of vastly different display types available to the designer, and they come in many sizes. There is no reason for this display type to be of the same typeface as the main body of the text, but of course it should not clash with it.

The title page is important: it can, as do the titles preceding a film, set the mood for the entire book. A serious, scholarly work will usually be best presented by a simple title page, soberly stating with dignified type the name of the book, the subtitle if there is one, the name of the author, the name of the publisher, and sometimes the date of first publication.

A biography or a work of history will often have a frontispiece—usually a photograph or map relevant to the text—facing the title page. The display face used for the title might attempt to create the period of history covered by the book, just as the typeface used throughout the text of the book will. The same applies to a novel, as well, although novels do not generally have pictorial frontispieces.

The variety of possible title pages is infinite—they can be serious or whimsical, strictly formal or engagingly informal. Above all, however, they give us the essential information about the book and present this information in a way appropriate to the book's contents.

The designer has choices, too, when it comes to part titles, although usually these will be presented simply—in a type size larger than that used for the main body of the text. When it comes to chapter titles and openings, however, the designer has more scope in which to work.

STAGES OF BOOK DESIGN

(design by Dana Sloan)

EDITOR'S REQUEST FOR DESIGN/LAYOUTS AND MANUFACTURING ESTIMATE

Title: WOMEN IN POLITICS (tentative)
Author: Ronna Romney and Beppie Harrison
Imprint: Crown Editor: Lisa Healy ISBN: ~~TK~~
Fiction: Non-illustrated nonfiction: X Illustrated nonfiction:
Trim size: 6 x 9 Estimated number of words: 272 ms pp Number of book pages wanted: 224
Retail price: ~~$17.95~~

Is there another book similar to this that we published? No
Is there another book by author and/or other publisher to follow for style? No
Text—set loose: Please bulk tight: (If a problem in fitting, only)

half title(s) x dedication x foreword appendix(es) x about the author
part titles contents x introduction index x glossary
ad card x list of illus. epigraph(s) footnotes other (describe)
title page x acknowledgments x author's note notes x
copyright page x preface bibliography running heads x

ILLUSTRATIONS IN TEXT (please give number of illustrations wherever applicable)
line: do we draw: who pays:
halftone: black-and-white photos: xerox: shoot from book:
other (describe):

ILLUSTRATIONS BIND SEPARATE (please give number of illustrations wherever applicable)
insert separate signature: wrap-around signature: center insert:
frontispiece: tip outside signature: other (describe):
no. pieces copy: photographs: transparencies: reflective art:
other (describe):
fees for this artwork: do we have to pay for prints:
any of this artwork unusually valuable:
total artwork fees we have paid to date:

ENDPAPERS plain: colored: x printed: if printed, what is copy:
do we draw it: who pays for it:

JACKET number of colors: 4 color type: x pictorial:
any special jacket fee(s) other than commissioned by art dept.:

BINDING (check 2) cloth: x paperback: sewed: unsewed: x

OFFSET If we are offsetting a previous/other-publisher edition of this book, please state:
trim size other edition: offset from printed sheets: film provided:
is film on order now: did you get film specs. from prod. dept.:
illustrations shoot from original copy: film provided: shoot book:
offset fee:
if you are changing other than title, copyright, jacket, binding spine, please state:

QUANTITY first printing cloth: 25M paper:
reprint cloth: 5M paper:

CONTRACT TERMS advance: $15,000 royalty rate: 10% on first 10,000; 12½% on next 5,000; 15% thereafter
any special notations on fees or schedule of delivery material in contract:

SUBSIDIARY RIGHTS POSSIBILITIES book clubs: x foreign sales: foreign run-on:
Estimated costs copyediting, proofreading: $750
Setting copy due to production: 10/6
Publication month: March 88
Layouts due: 7/17 LH 5/28

NOTE: Sample pages will be set only if unusual copy or other special considerations. If so, please state:

1. Editor's request with specifications

3. Sketches

11:10

By observing deuterium emissions with a radio telescope, we can determine its abundance relative to normal hydrogen. The ratio of the two is a sensitive indicator of the conditions in the universe at the time of the isotope's creation.

Deuterium has been discovered in various molecules in place of normal hydrogen, and both radio and ultraviolet emissions of deuterium atoms have been recorded. ~~and~~ Although there does not appear to be evidence in the deuterium observations of sufficient mass to close the universe, astronomers now believe that there is much mass hidden within clusters of galaxies ~~(Figure 11.9)~~ and in invisible halos around galaxies ~~(Figure 11.10)~~.

What does all this mean for star formation? If the universe continues to expand forever, eventually star formation will come to an end, and galaxies will grow cold and dark. If, on the other hand, the universe is closed, the expansion will someday stop, and as the universe plunges headlong back toward its origins, the universe will heat up as it grows smaller, and stars will continue to form out of gas and dust until the moment when all the matter in the universe is crushed out of existence into the biggest black hole of all and, perhaps, a new universe will rise from the corpse of the old.

(A) A SENSE OF THE FUTURE ~~[illegible]~~

We do not know all there is to know about the life and death of stars. We will see new vistas from satellites as we probe the inner recesses of dark clouds in space, and astronomers will continue to look for the tell-tale signs of black holes in orbit about visual stars.

Yet even though there is much to learn, we have witnessed tremendous strides in understanding the cosmos. Some techniques are still in their infancy, such as observation of gamma rays, but astronomers have used every part of the electromagnetic spectrum to garner information about celestial objects, and as we have outlined in this book, the general story appears complete, with plenty

2. Read and review the manuscript

COMPOSITION SPECIFICATIONS CROWN • WESTOVER • BARRE • POTTER ONE PARK AVENUE, NEW YORK 10016

To ____ Date Oct 23 Title Momentum: Women in American Politics Now
Imprint Crown Author ~~Romney and Harrison~~
Prod. Sup. Kay Riley Editor Lisa Healy Designer Dana Sloan
Illustrations: B&W Line — B&W Halftone — Color —
Char. Per Line 64 Char. Per Page 2496 Total FM 8 pgs. Total Pages 224
Lines Per Page 39 Total Char. 504,043 Total Text 216
Trim Size 6 x 9 Type Page Size includes r.h. & folio ____ x ____ Picas. Margins: Head 5½ pi to text Gutter 5½ pi

Body Matter	Type Face	Size	Sink	Space Ab. & Bel.	Indent
Text	Electra	11/13 x 25½ pi			
Par. Indent	1 em.				
Left R.H.	Helvetica Heavy U+lc	8 pt.		3½ pi sink from trim	ctr.
Copy	Book title				
Right R.H.	same as left r.h.				
Copy	Chapt title				
Folios	Electra	11 pt		3½ pi from bottom trim	dropped ctr.
Ch. Opening Folio	same as above.				
Part No.	none				
Part Title	none				
Chap. No.	Anzeigen Bold followed by 15pt box	48 pt		5½ pi sink	fl. L
Chap. Title	Anzeigen Bold U+lc TNT	48 pt 48/48		5½ pi sink	5 pi from left
Sub Title	none				
space breaks	2 l# with 3 6pt boxes centered on #, 2½ pi between boxes.				
(A) hds (Notes)	Helvetica Heavy U+lc	11 pt		1 l# above	fl. L
Opening Style	Chapt ops. 27 lines per normal page				
Extract					
Notes	Electra	11/13 x 25½ pi		set turnovers with hanging indent	
Captions	none				
Poetry	none				
Footnotes	none				
Index	tk.				
Glossary	none				
Bibliography	none				

4. Specification sheet for the typesetter

5. Ronna Romne Harrison

hetic design? Why do the pace-makers in the art of printing rave over a specific face of type? What do they see in it? Why is it so superlatively pleasant to their eyes? Good design is always practical design. And what they see in a good type design is, partly, its excellent practical fitness to perform its work. It has a "heft" and balance in all of its parts just right for its size,as any good tool has. Your good chair has all of its parts made nicely to the right size to do exactly the work that the chair has to do neither clumsy and thick, nor "skinny" and weak no waste of material and no lack of strength. And, beyond that, the chair may have been made by a man who worked out in his sense of fine shapes and curves and proportions it may be, actually a work of art.

The same thing holds for shapes of letters. And your chair, or your letter (if a true artist made it) will have, besides its good looks, a suitability to the nth degree to be sat in, or stamped on paper and read. That explains, in a way, why the experts rave over the fine shapes of letters; but it fails to explain wherein the shapes are fine. If you seek to go further with the inquiry, theories will be your only answer. Here is a theory that the proponent thinks may have sense in it: Fine type letters were, in the first place, copies of fine written letters.

How is one to assess and evaluate a type face in terms of its esthetic design? Why do the pace-makers in the art of printing rave over a specific face of type? What do they see in it? Why is it so superlatively pleasant to their eyes? Good design is always practical

90

5. Sample pages

BPE GRAPHICS
OUR JOB # CJG0824
YOUR JOB # 6052
GALLEY # 4
REVISION # 1
DATE SUBMITTED 8/26

Women among Men

wants to make a career is that she keep her eye on the ball and recognize that a career does not mean a cocktail suit. And that is where I think women in this town very clearly fall into two categories, the workers and the partyers. I don't disagree that work can get done giving dinner parties. But before someone determines that she wants to move into a career mode in Washington, D.C., as a female, she should know herself well enough to know where she wants to go. This is not only a power town. This town also has a higher incidence of alcoholism than any other town in the United States of America. The alcohol circuit in this town is atrocious. I hear about the business that's done at the cocktail parties, but I don't buy that. I just don't think you get business done in the barrooms. I happen to think that people do not think clearly when they're drinking— they may be very agreeable to what you're saying, and the next day you call to seal the deal and they have memory block. Everybody has a different approach. The way I deal is I work during business hours or when the Congress is in session."

Michelle Laxalt is not the only woman to decide that some ways of doing business are counterproductive. June Roselle has raised money for Detroit's powerful Mayor Coleman Young for fourteen years and is one of his most important political appointees, but for somewhat different reasons she figures that as a woman, she does better to do her talking with the mayor on a one-to-one basis, rather than joining in the late-night meetings at his official residence with the male inner circle. "If I were to call up the mayor and say I really think I should be in at those meetings, I think he'd probably put me in. But then they'd all be uncomfortable. Because most of them are older men, and they talk foul, and they look at me as so prim and proper. I mean, the mayor does not swear in front of me, and if he does, he says 'Excuse me.' Again, it's the age. He looks at me as the mother of these children [she has five], and as a very respectable, genteel type of person. I think he likes that idea, that I am like I am, and that I'm his fund-raiser because he thinks people are always so surprised when they meet me that '*you* work for Coleman Young?' I think he likes that. But again, there is something to that old boys' network. I'm sure that when they sit over there they're drinking and talking about where the city should go and there are many, many serious conversations going on. But I imagine I'd be very uncomfortable in it."

6. Galleys

5. Women among Men

It was one of the first big events of Reagan's 1984 reelection campaign, and the president and Mrs. Reagan were being ushered to their places on the gigantic podium facing the crowd. The first lady's radiant public smile froze momentarily as she looked around the podium at all the beaming politicians—the beaming *male* politicians—who were going to be surrounding the president, chosen for their local importance to bathe in reflected glory. But this was the year of the gender gap, the year when the Democrats had a woman on the ticket, the year when the Republican party was going to need to broaden its appeal to women, and on that commodious platform not a single women was to be seen. It was the Republican establishment in all its masculine glory. The wife of the president—accredited only by her relationship to a man—was going to be the sole woman there.

Nancy Reagan blew up discreetly but unmistakably. Nobody may have noticed the omission before, but they noticed it then. Indeed, Mrs. Reagan was so furious that campaign staffers carefully found seats for themselves at a safe distance, out of earshot of irate whispers. Immediately after the event came a memo from campaign manager Jim Baker, ordering that from then on 50 percent of the people on every dais would be women, no matter what. It wasn't always easy: in some of the particularly chauvinistic areas the powerful men who had to be excluded in favor of women well down the totem pole put up a fight to try to retain their position, but every time, when Mrs. Reagan swept her glance over the platform, the women were there. The men running the presidential campaign

102

Women among Men

who simply hadn't noticed their absence before had been educated, at least temporarily.

• • •

Few men begin to understand how hard it is for a woman to make her way in the political world.

"Sometimes there are men who are honestly oblivious," explained Monica McFadden, formerly executive director of the National Women's Political Caucus. "Let me give you a perfect example: California's senator Alan Cranston. It does not compute in this man's mind whether the person sitting across from him is male or female. You're either qualified and competent or you're not. If you aren't, he will pay no attention to you. If you are, it doesn't matter. But there are all the others though who don't know because we're invisible to them and what they see is a male world and if a female voice pipes up they don't hear it. Those men range in age from eighteen to seventy-nine. I know a lot of men I've sat near, where I can say something and the man next to me can say exactly the same thing and he's the one that's heard. Why? Because I'm a woman. The pitch of the voice is wrong or whatever."

Among male politicians, just as among the male population in general, there is a bedrock level of a very few individuals who honestly believe that politics and government in general is something that women ought not to mess around with. Seldom do they give much indication of having their minds open to intelligent discussion on the topic: their opinion is apparently integrally linked with their view of the essential nature of mankind and the universe. Most of them are older men; many of them have come far enough to learn that it is imprudent to say what they think openly, at least in public, which is probably as far toward understanding women's ambitions as they're ever going to get. Basically, that unconvertable bedrock level is not the problem. (For one thing, according to pollster Harrison Hickman, there is a balancing 8–10 percent of the population who prefer to vote for—or, presumably, pay attention to—a woman.) According to most women, the problem lies in the vastly greater numbers of more aware, more sympathetic men who nonetheless have no appreciation of the extent to which women have been closed out of political power.

"There are still massive perceptual problems," Celinda Lake of

103

7. Final pages

The chapter title can carry out the spirit of the book, but, first of all, the designer must keep in mind the length of each title. Whether the length of each can be kept to one line, or whether two or even more lines will be needed, will help decide what typeface and size to use. In any case, of course, these titles will be printed in a typeface considerably larger than that used in the text. They will sometimes consist of all capital letters and sometimes capitals and lower case. Most chapter titles are simply designed, but from time to time a designer will want to carry out a decorative motif from the title page.

Because the display type used for chapter titles is usually placed lower than the top of the normal type page, the designer must precisely designate the placement of the chapter title. The distance between the top of the page and the chapter title is called the sinkage, and the amount or depth of sinkage is stated in terms of picas.

More decisions must be made by the designer, such as the selection and placing of page numbers, or folios, and the design of the running heads. These will be largely dictated by the kind of typeface used in the main body of the text.

Once the designer has decided on the typeface, he or she will prepare a precise castoff, or character count, which gives the number of characters in the manuscript. This is an exacting but essential job, made easier if the manuscript is clean and well typed, and if the same typewriter is used throughout. Each letter, number, punctuation mark, and space is considered as one unit in this count. The most accurate way of counting the number of units or characters would be to simply count them one by one. This would give the precise length of the manuscript, but obviously it would be impractical. Instead, designers use a somewhat less exact method.

Garamond
Garamond Italic

Picas / Size	10	12	14	16	18	20	22	24	26	28	30
6	40	48	56	64	72	80	88	96	104	112	120
7	38	46	53	61	68	76	84	91	99	107	114
8	35	42	49	56	63	70	77	84	91	98	105
9	33	40	46	53	59	66	73	79	86	92	99
10	30	36	42	48	54	60	66	72	78	84	90
11	28	34	39	45	50	56	62	67	73	78	84
12	26	31	36	42	47	52	57	62	68	73	78
14	22	26	31	35	40	44	48	53	57	62	66
16	19	23	27	30	34	38	42	46	49	53	57
18	18	22	25	29	32	36	40	43	46	50	54
20	15	18	21	24	27	30	33	36	39	42	45
24	13	16	18	21	23	26	29	31	34	36	39

Chart for casting off Garamond

They count the characters in several lines of the manuscript and thus arrive at an average number of characters per line. Then, the average number of lines per page can be calculated, and the number of characters per line times the number of lines per page will give a fair idea of the number of characters per page. (No such approximation is necessary for manuscripts prepared on a computer, for the computer provides a precise character count.)

There are several more decisions a designer must make. One involves the area of the type page—its width and length. This includes only the area on which the text will be printed and not the margins. This decision is dictated by appearance, economic factors, and readability. The margins are, of course, determined by the size of the type area, the margins being in a sense the frame for the text.

Appearance means simply what would look best for a given text, while the economic factor concerns the desired

Aldus PageMaker computer system

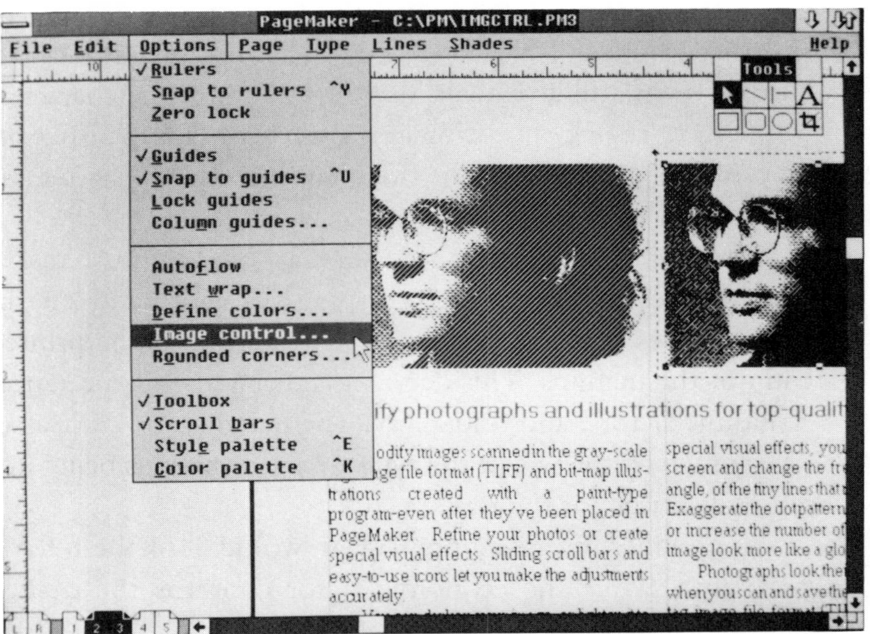

Screen while working with PageMaker, allowing the type and photos to be seen at the same time. Insert is the menu of design options

GO FROM START TO FINISH IN 4 STEPS.

1. Begin your publication by preparing text, illustrations and graphics.

Write and edit all your copy with a standard word processing program, choosing type specifications as you go. Create illustrations and graphics using a scanner or any of the popular computer graphics programs.

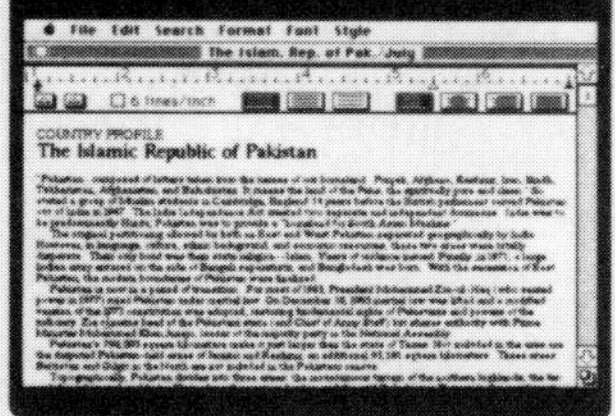

2. Next, develop a format for your publication with PageMaker's master page feature.

Define the margins, the number of columns and the column widths. Then add standing design elements like column rules, bars, screens, boxes, headers and you're ready to go. PageMaker lets you modify individual page formats any time you choose.

3. Now, bring your text or illustration into PageMaker, position the pointer and click your mouse button.

PageMaker fills a column with typeset text, then allows you to flow the remaining copy to another column or page. You can also crop or proportionally scale your graphics to fit any space. On-screen rulers and guidelines help you put everything in its place with ease and accuracy.

4. Once the pages look the way you want, you're ready to print.

Laser printer output makes excellent camera-ready art for most applications. PageMaker output can also be easily integrated with conventional production techniques to include black and white and four-color photos, high-resolution art, oversize pages, overlays, spot-color and special graphics effects.

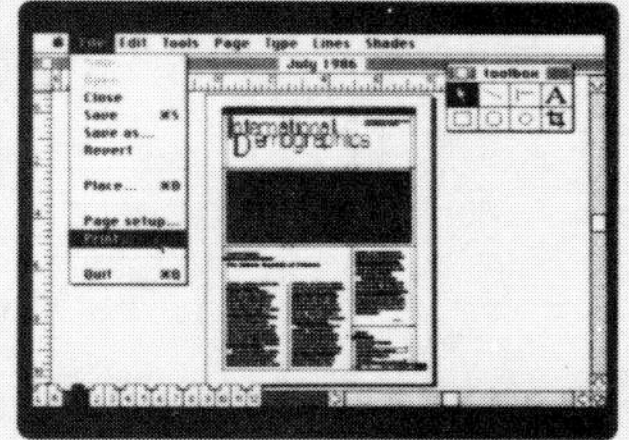

Four steps of designing with PageMaker

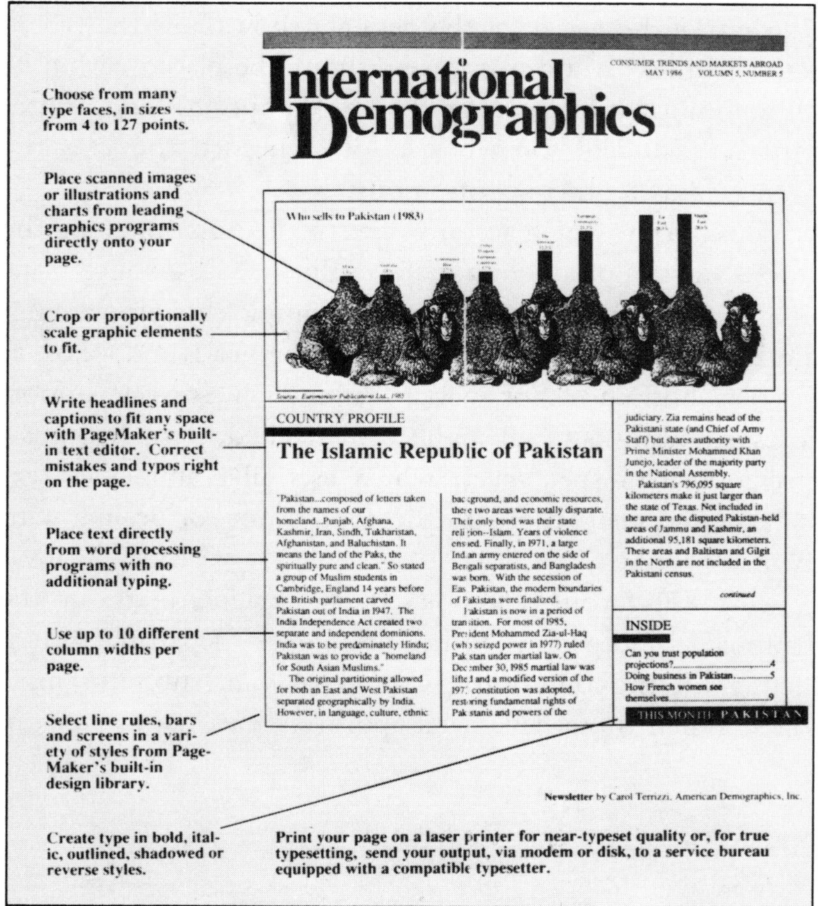

CONSUMER TRENDS AND MARKETS ABROAD
MAY 1986 VOLUMN 5, NUMBER 5

International Demographics

Who sells to Pakistan (1983)

Source: Euromonitor Publications Ltd., 1985

COUNTRY PROFILE

The Islamic Republic of Pakistan

"Pakistan...composed of letters taken from the names of our homeland...Punjab, Afghana, Kashmir, Iran, Sindh, Tukharistan, Afghanistan, and Baluchistan. It means the land of the Paks, the spiritually pure and clean." So stated a group of Muslim students in Cambridge, England 14 years before the British parliament carved Pakistan out of India in 1947. The India Independence Act created two separate and independent dominions. India was to be predominately Hindu; Pakistan was to provide a "homeland for South Asian Muslims."

The original partitioning allowed for both an East and West Pakistan separated geographically by India. However, in language, culture, ethnic background, and economic resources, these two areas were totally disparate. Their only bond was their state religion--Islam. Years of violence ensued. Finally, in 1971, a large Indian army entered on the side of Bengali separatists, and Bangladesh was born. With the secession of East Pakistan, the modern boundaries of Pakistan were finalized.

Pakistan is now in a period of transition. For most of 1985, President Mohammed Zia-ul-Haq (who seized power in 1977) ruled Pakistan under martial law. On December 30, 1985 martial law was lifted and a modified version of the 1973 constitution was adopted, restoring fundamental rights of Pakistanis and powers of the judiciary. Zia remains head of the Pakistani state (and Chief of Army Staff) but shares authority with Prime Minister Mohammed Khan Junejo, leader of the majority party in the National Assembly.

Pakistan's 796,095 square kilometers make it just larger than the state of Texas. Not included in the area are the disputed Pakistan-held areas of Jammu and Kashmir, an additional 95,181 square kilometers. These areas and Baltistan and Gilgit in the North are not included in the Pakistani census.

continued

INSIDE

THIS MONTH: PAKISTAN

Newsletter by Carol Terrizzi, American Demographics, Inc.

Choose from many type faces, in sizes from 4 to 127 points.
Place scanned images or illustrations and charts from leading graphics programs directly onto your page.
Crop or proportionally scale graphic elements to fit.
Write headlines and captions to fit any space with PageMaker's built-in text editor. Correct mistakes and typos right on the page.
Place text directly from word processing programs with no additional typing.
Use up to 10 different column widths per page.
Select line rules, bars and screens in a variety of styles from PageMaker's built-in design library.
Create type in bold, italic, outlined, shadowed or reverse styles.
Print your page on a laser printer for near-typeset quality or, for true typesetting, send your output, via modem or disk, to a service bureau equipped with a compatible typesetter.

Some of the many things that can be done with PageMaker

length of the book; the more words per page, the fewer pages required, and thus the less paper. As for readability, it has been shown that the human eye can most easily span a line that has no more than sixty-five to seventy characters in it.

The width of the characters of each typeface differs, and a designer designates the width of the line of type in picas. The other common measure in typography is the point. There are approximately seventy-two points to an inch and twelve points to a pica. Thus, a pica equals about one-sixth of an inch. The rulers used by designers show picas on one edge and inches on the other.

Once the design has been completed, the designer transmits the plans onto sheets of a special drawing paper. This is called the layout. After ruling off the exact size of the trimmed page and of the text area, the designer shows how the type—both main text and display faces—should be placed within it. All the information necessary for the compositor and printer must be included; the typeface for each part, the size, the leading, and all other specifications.

This layout, which accompanies the manuscript along the various steps of production, will usually include detailed plans for all of the front and back matter; a sample chapter opening; and two facing pages of text with running heads and folios, as well as specifications for special matter such as extracts, footnotes, subheads, and subsubheads. Attached to the layout is a specification or spec sheet, which lists all examples of text material and instructions to the compositor for dealing with them.

Once this layout is completed, the designer marks up the manuscript and gives it to the production department. It is then sent to the compositor, who prepares and submits sample pages. When those have been approved, the manuscript can go into production. However, the designer's job is not finished. Often, he or she will consult with the production supervisor concerning the choice of paper, and in all cases, the designer follows the book along its various stages to see that the plans have been faithfully carried out.

In addition, before the book is actually printed, the designer may be called upon to prepare or supervise a mechanical to be used for platemaking. A mechanical is the final assembly of all elements of each page of the book. It is prepared according to indications that show the precise way each page should look; everything that is to go into the book will be shown or indicated on the mechanical. Precision and neatness are essential, since all the elements in their correct positions will be photographed, and the films will serve to make the plates used in printing the book.

The first step in making the mechanical is usually ruling an artboard, a special sheet of heavy white cardboard, for page size, trim size, and placement of "bleeding" photographs that will extend to one or more of the trimmed edges of the page. This ruling is done in a special light blue, a color not picked up by the camera.

Reproduction or repro proofs (final, corrected proofs printed on specially treated paper) are cut up and carefully pasted on the board with rubber cement or wax. Running heads and folios, too, are pasted in their correct positions, with extreme care being taken with spacing and margins.

As for illustrations, line images—which appear in the book as a solid color—can be pasted in with the type copy, but continuous tone or halftone copy, which contains shadings and must first be photographed through a screen, cannot be pasted on the mechanical. Instead, blank spaces, with a key to the illustration that will fill each of these spaces on the film,

She is a female harbor seal, heavy with her first pup. She has come out of the water to give birth.

Away from other seals, the new pup comes into the world. Mother and pup touch noses and call to each other, learning each other's smells and sounds. Briefly, the pup nurses on her mother's rich milk and sleeps by her side.

As the tide comes in, the newborn follows her mother into the ocean. Newborn harbor seal pups have little insulating fat, so they cannot stay long in the chilly water. The pup waits on the beach in the sun while her mother slips into the sea to feed.

A mechanical page

will be left. These halftone illustrations are inserted after a film has been made of the mechanical.

Today, a good desktop publishing computer software system—examples are Ventura, Aldus PageMaker, and Quark XPress—can be both a creative aid and a time-saver to a book designer. With the use of these systems, designers can do castoffs, page layouts, spec sheets, and even sample pages right in their offices. When working with electronic manuscripts, designers can put typesetting instructions directly onto the floppy disks. This done, the disks can go directly to the typesetter; no retyping will be necessary before the type is set. This results in a saving of both time and money; it also reduces the number of typesetting errors.

A designer's job requires creative as well as technical skills. Inspiration and imagination are essential, as is a great deal of hard work. It is rewarding work, however, since good design can contribute considerably to the success of a book.

THE JACKET DESIGNER

Largely because of its effectiveness in selling a book, great importance is placed on the design of the book jacket. Originally, the jacket—a heavier than usual paper wrapped around the book—served largely as protection against dirt, dust, and grease. Today, the jacket has another, more important function. No longer merely a protective wrapper, it is used to attract readers and to identify the book, both by its graphic design and by what is written on it. It is, in a sense, an advertisement for the book as well as a quick source of information about it; it might be likened to a poster, wrapped around a book. For these reasons, great attention must be paid not only to the artwork to be used on a jacket, but to the written information that is printed on it.

A successful book jacket is eye-catching, legible, and informative. It must, first of all, attract the professional book buyer, that is, the bookstore owner. This person usually sees the front of the jacket long before seeing the book itself, and orders copies of the book on the basis of its jacket as well as the sales representative's presentation. Next, the jacket must catch the eye of customers browsing through a bookstore. Many potential readers, looking for a book to read or to give, will be drawn to a book on display by its jacket, bypassing the books with nondescript jackets for those with attractive ones. They will then read what is written on the jacket flaps and, on the basis of that, make their decision. Another factor that might be kept in mind when a jacket is designed is whether or not it will photograph well, for a photo could be useful for a catalog or for advertising. Many books become known through eye-catching jackets that "identify" them for the reader.

The designer of the jacket is generally chosen by the publishing house's art director, who helps develop and maintain a style for the publishing house and who has a good idea of the kind of jacket wanted for each book. With this in mind, the art director will give the assignment on the basis of a jacket designer's past work. Considerations in choosing a jacket designer include whether that designer is most comfortable with illustrations, which might be done by another artist, or with photographs, or is especially imaginative in the use of type.

The conception of the book jacket necessarily takes a longer time than the actual execution because it is the conception that involves a creative act, one requiring thought, imagination, flair, and a sympathetic understanding of the book. The execution itself is largely a matter of mechanical skill, although this skill might be of great importance if a complicated illustration is involved. Preparation of the jacket mechanical is as complex and demanding as that of any book illustration.

At the very beginning, the jacket designer will discuss the

Design by Tom Stvan

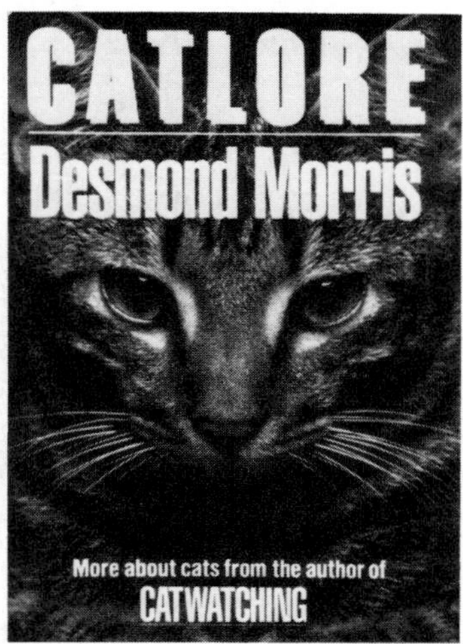

Design by Dana Sloan
Photo by Richard Riley

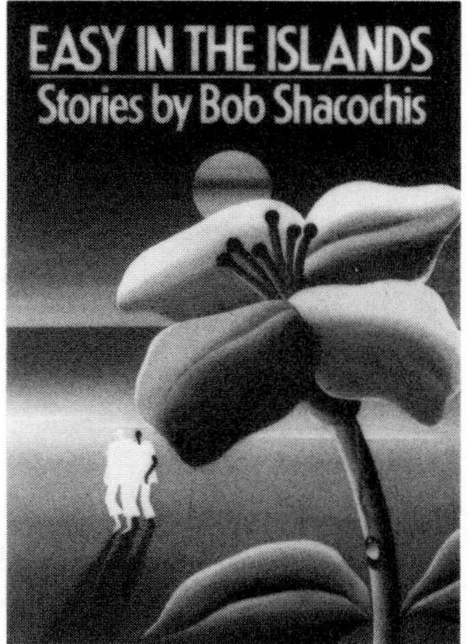

Design by James K. Davis
Illustration by Alain Gauthier

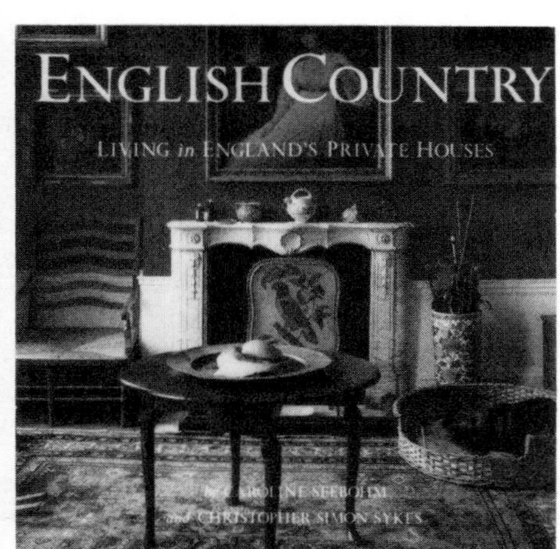

Design by Gael Towey
Photo by Christopher Simon Sykes

Design by John Grandits
Illustration by David Small

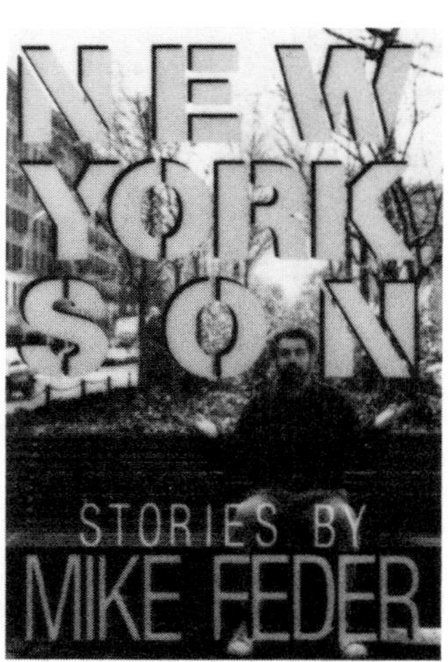

Photo by Jillian LeVine

job with the art director. The latter will have suggestions as to how the jacket should look and will know the size required as well as the budget for the jacket. The amount of money that can be spent will determine the number of colors that the designer will be allowed to use. Following that, a conference with the editor of the book may be useful to the designer as will, of course, a reading of the manuscript.

In addition, the designer will need to be told exactly what written matter, or copy, will be placed on the jacket. The front of the jacket will certainly contain the title of the book and the name of the author. The length of the title and the length of the author's name will necessarily influence the choice of type. A quote from a well-known critic, or a line such as "by the author of. . . ," which will then mention the title of an earlier successful book by the same author, could be included to identify the author whose name might be less well known than that of his or her previous book.

On the spine of the jacket, the designer will work out the placement of the title of the book, the author's name, and the name of the publishing house. This is important because the book might be displayed on a bookshelf where only the spine would show rather than on a table or in a window where the front of the jacket would be visible.

The back of the jacket might contain written material—a description of the book or biographical information about the author—or a photograph of the author, or merely decorative matter. The two flaps, the ends of the jacket which fold inside the front and back covers of the volume, will generally show the price and give information about the contents of the book and/or about the author.

If the editor of the book feels that the author's name is of special importance, this information must be given to the

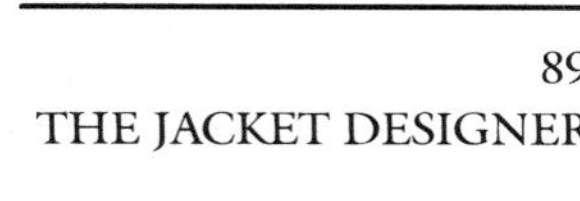

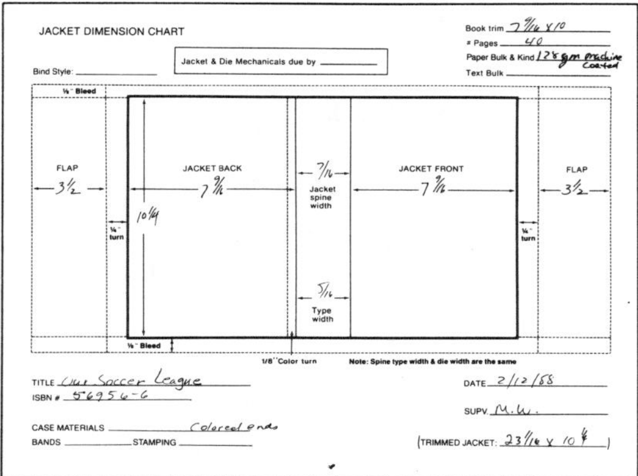

JACKET DIMENSION CHART

Bind Style: ______

Jacket & Die Mechanicals due by ______

Book trim 7 9/16 x 10
Pages 40
Paper Bulk & Kind 128 gm machine coated
Text Bulk ______

1/8" Bleed				
FLAP	JACKET BACK	7/16 Jacket spine width	JACKET FRONT	FLAP
3 1/2	7 9/16		7 9/16	3 1/2
1/4" turn	10 1/4	5/16 Type width		1/4" turn
1/8" Bleed				

1/8" Color turn

Note: Spine type width & die width are the same

TITLE Our Soccer League
ISBN # 56956-6
DATE 2/12/88
SUPV. M.W.
CASE MATERIALS ______ Colored ends
BANDS ______ STAMPING ______
(TRIMMED JACKET: 23 1/16 x 10 1/4)

Jacket dimension chart

Mechanical for a jacket

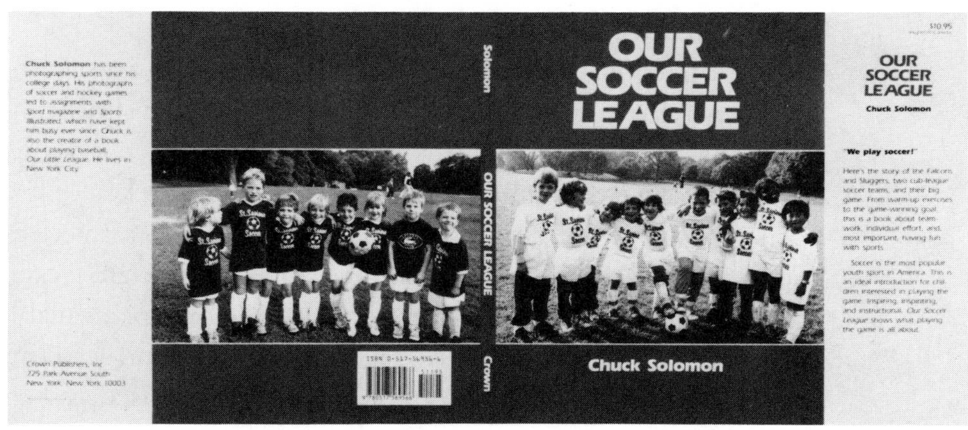

Finished jacket

STAGES OF JACKET DESIGN
(Art direction by James K. Davis, Illustration by Michael Garland)

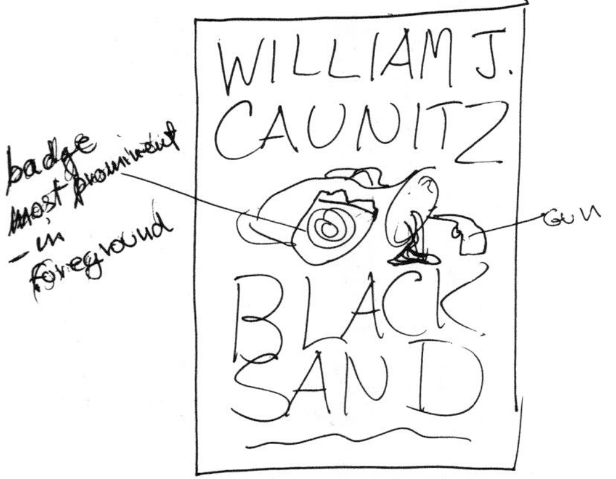

1. *Thumbnail given by the art director to the designer*

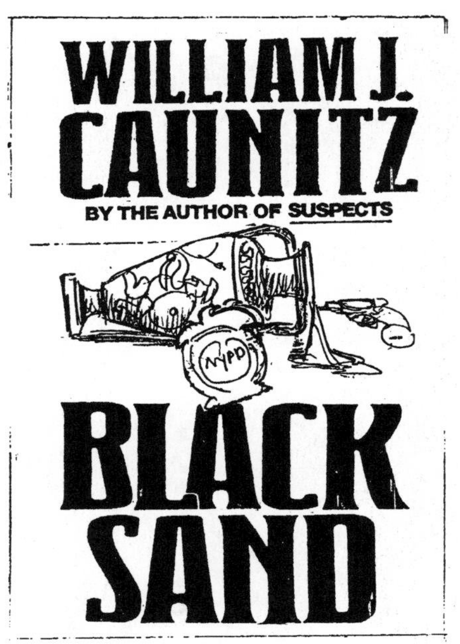

2. *Designer's sketch*

designer; if, instead, the title of the book should be emphasized, the designer must be informed. In other words, before beginning the job, the jacket designer must have every possible piece of information that will help to create a successful book jacket.

Once the designer has all this information, it is time to begin thinking about the jacket. It is at this point that inspiration comes into play. All we have to do to see the infinite variety of book jackets possible is to spend a short time in a bookstore or in a library looking at books. Each designer has had to face the same problem of creating a jacket that is both faithful to the content of the book and will attract the reader's attention. The solutions are endless. There are jackets that use type alone—and the different kinds of type available for display are very many, to say nothing of hand-lettering designed for a specific jacket. Photographs are used, as are

3. *Final painting*

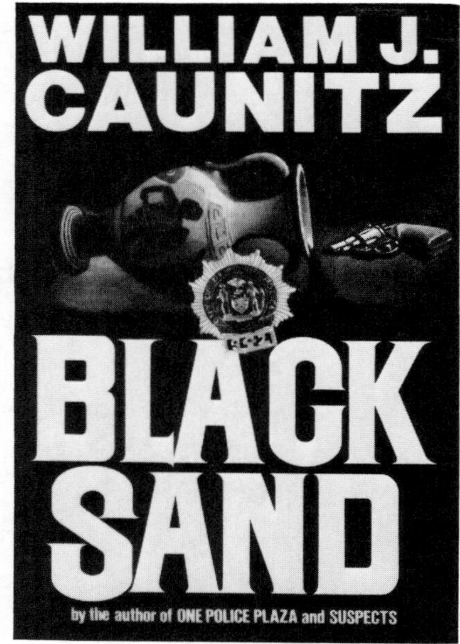

4. *Comp submitted by designer*

collages, montages, drawings, paintings, and decorative patterns. Jackets can be stark; they can be florid; they can be dramatic or humorous, directly informative or strongly evocative.

Faced with all these choices, but limited by the budget and the nature of the book, the designer must find what seems to be the best approach, the one that will satisfy the needs of the book and the taste of the public.

Several solutions could come to mind, in which case the designer makes sketches of the best of these ideas. From these sketches, the designer chooses two or more ideas and makes a "comp," a tightly drawn color sketch of the design. These comps are then brought to the publishing house, where the ideas are debated among the staff. The art director, of course, will have a say. The editor, too, is bound to have strong feelings and probably suggestions. However, perhaps the decisive opinion will come from the sales department, since the jacket's primary function is to sell books. The jacket is generally the sales reps' only visual tool in selling a book to a bookseller; they cannot possibly carry copies of each book that they are selling, so—except in special cases where the overall appearance of the book is an important factor—they will sell solely on the strength of the jacket or a proof of that jacket. The jacket's look is therefore of great importance—almost equal to that of the advertising budget or promotion plans when the reps try to place the largest number of copies of a book in the stores.

Because they are better acquainted with bookselling than are most other members of the publishing house—because they are closer to the marketplace—the sales reps' opinion should be carefully considered. It is not unusual for a jacket to be enthusiastically accepted by the art and editorial departments and then rejected by the sales department on commercial grounds. There is, of course, no reason for a jacket to be in poor taste or unfaithful to the contents of the book. Yet the book jacket has become a sales tool, and as such its commercial value is primary.

From the number of comps submitted, one will prove most acceptable to the art, editorial, and sales departments. Members of each department may well have suggestions for improvements, and with all of these in mind, the jacket designer will know exactly how to proceed. The designer can now begin work on the mechanical for the jacket, that is, execute the design from which the final jacket will be printed. This is precision work, and it is essential that the exact format of the book as well as its bulk be known, so that the jacket will—as it must—fit comfortably around the finished book. Once the mechanical is completed, the jacket is ready for printing. (The actual printing of a jacket will be discussed in the chapter on the color printer.)

No one can say whether a jacket is good or bad. There are esthetic judgments, and these are of some value. But many people in publishing say that the successful jacket is the one that has been wrapped around the book that sells. To the jacket designer, this may seem to be a cynical attitude, but perhaps it is the most realistic of all.

THE PRODUCTION SUPERVISOR

Modern technology has advanced so rapidly in recent years that methods of book production today differ radically from those of just a few decades ago; by the same token, today's methods will most likely be altered and even outdated a few years from now. Nonetheless, the goal of book production remains and will remain the same: to transform a manuscript into a printed and bound book within a specific time and budget.

The person responsible for planning and keeping track of that transformation is the production supervisor. This person must have a solid background in all phases of book production and must keep up with technological advances. It is essential, too, for the production supervisor to know the advantages and the shortcomings of the available suppliers, for it is his or her job to select the compositor, the printer, and the binder and to choose the paper to be used, as well as the cover materials to be used for the case of each book. Since many books will be in production at the same time—and at different stages—the job has always been a complicated one, involving the selection of each supplier, the control of the supplier's materials or work, and coordination of the schedules of a large number of suppliers and craftsmen. Today, it is even more complicated since much work—such as color separation, printing, and binding—is often (especially in the case of illustrated books) done outside the United States. Among the most common of these foreign sources are Japan, Hong Kong, Italy, England, Spain, Belgium, and the Netherlands.

The production supervisor, too, acts as a liaison between the publishing house and the various suppliers. He or she can advise an editor, in the preliminary stages, as to the feasibility of doing a certain book at a reasonable price. There are times when an editor would like to go ahead with a project, but feels it would cost too much to do because of production complexities. Consultation with the production supervisor could make the editor aware of the alternate options of printing a book, thus enabling it to be produced in the right way and at an economical price.

It is most important for the production supervisor to keep in mind the possible conflict between budget restrictions and the quality desired. He or she will most likely know where to go for the best possible printing and binding, but that knowledge is not enough; the production supervisor's job is not only to have the job done well, but to have it done within the limitations of the budget for any given book. The printer or binder who might do the finest job could be too expensive, so the production supervisor must be in touch with other, less expensive printers or binders who can do an acceptable job if carefully checked and supervised. For each solution, there must be an alternate and today, to obtain the best price, a production supervisor must be well informed about printers, binders, and paper mills in many parts of the world.

It is essential that the production supervisor be on good working terms with a number of suppliers and know which would be best suited for each book. Several factors are involved in this choice. Knowledge of each supplier's equipment is essential in determining that supplier's capability to do a given job. The supplier's reliability in maintaining a high quality of work is vital, as is the supplier's reliability when it comes to keeping to a schedule. The production supervisor must know which supplier will be available at which time, and which will understand the needs of the publisher, as well as the possibilities and limitations of the printer and binder involved in any given project.

Quality is, obviously, of great importance, but one of the first tasks of the production supervisor, after receiving the manuscript, is to obtain cost estimates from several different suppliers. Since different suppliers charge different amounts for their work, these estimates will usually have to be obtained from several suppliers before a decision can be made.

Book publishers work on a very small margin of profit, and for this reason it is most important that the publisher know just how much each book will cost. A publisher sells most of its books at 60 percent of their retail price. Approximately 10 percent of that retail price is paid to the author and there are other expenses, such as overhead (which includes salaries, rent, telephone, warehouse costs, and office supplies), publicity, advertising, and so on. The cost of the actual production of the book will be at least 20 percent of the retail price, so there remains very little, if any, profit on a book that sells only moderately well. Obviously, then, an error in a production estimate can be financially disastrous; a miscalculation, an

Be sure to list name of supplier for all manufacturing

PLANT COST BO________ List________ BB________

COMP	AA's/EA's	} 1000
	Text Harry's Mad (128pp) + $350	
	Capts.	400
	Index, rh, heads, misc.	200
	Display	
	Cop Ed & Prfrd	200
	Jkt. fronts & flaps	350
ART	Text design dummy 350 @ $13 pg = 288	638
	Text mech. @ $5 pg = 480 + 100 cx	580
	Design, dummy, mech. Jacket & Insert	500
PREP	Camera & Plates	339
	Strip illus. @ 14 –	280
	~~Make Ready~~	
	Shoot line & h.t.	
	Sig ✓ prep, proof	1000
	~~Ht.~~ final pl. & blue	100
	Cov. prep & blue	
	Color seps. & pfs.	
	Insert Strip & pl. Permission fees	2000
	~~Stats &~~ blues 45 + 100 cx	145
MISC	Dies	—
	Slipcase/Box/Mech. Bds.	150
	Other Cover Art	500
	TOTAL PLANT	8600 ~~8282~~

Ptg #: 1 Impt: 053 ISBN #: ________ DATE ________

W.F. # ________ OK Mach ________ Final ________ From ________

Title First Book of Baseball (Trade)

Price: Cloth $9.95 Paper ________

Trim 5¼" x 8" Text Pages 96 Forms ________

Insert # Pages ________ Forms ________ # Seps ________

Halftones 20 Line ________

Text # Colors ________ Imposition ________

Paper 22¾" rolls : 70# /M 36.21

P+S Regular Offset

Paper stocked: ____ on hand: ____ Must buy: ____ Same as before: ____

Stock size actually needed ________

Waste: Quote ____ Scale ____ Average % ____ Paper Price figured as: net+ ____ %

10 M Sheets 4381 # @ .47¢

____ M Sheets ____ # @ ____

____ M Sheets ____ # @ ____

Binding Specs Last bound at Bindery #5M roll price

Case & Mtls. PRTD film lam case

~~On hand~~ Jkts. None Inserts ________ Covers ________

Sewing Burst Inside bulk ¼" Lining Up: ________

Ends White Text # Page/Sig ________

Boards 110 pasted Back Round Bands Yes

Illustrations Bind As ________ Stamp —

		QUANTITY	QUANTITY	QUANTITY
		10,000		
	TOTAL PLANT	.8600 ✓		
SHEET	Text paper 2060 ✓	.2060 ✓		
	Text pw mr Fairfield	.0971		
	Insert paper			
	Insert pw			
COST	End pw & stock			
	Cover 4/0 ~~Jkt~~ pw & stock Phoenix (no jacket)	.1377		
	Cov. pw & stock			
	Component Sheet } freight	.0260		
	Bind–FOB Avenel Fairfield	.4934		
	TOTAL MFG. COST	1.8202 ✓		
	Storage	.0300		
	List entire rate: ROYALTY RATE 8% Scioren	.7960 ✓		
	TOTAL COST	2.6462 ✓		
	Break even:	(26.59)		

Production estimate

added expense, or a forgotten detail can easily mean the difference between profit and loss on any one title.

This cost estimate must take into account every facet of production. It is divided into two main parts: plant costs and manufacturing costs. Plant costs are costs that occur only once, no matter how many copies of the book are printed. These plant costs include design work, composition—the setting of all type for both the book and the jacket, proofs, mechanicals, and artwork for the book and jacket, plates, and binding dies. The more copies of each title printed, the lower the cost of these items per copy, since these nonrecurring costs will be divided by a larger figure.

Manufacturing costs, on the other hand, are those that depend on the number of copies of each book that are printed and bound. The manufacturing costs include paper, binding, and presswork—although printing a larger quantity at one time will reduce the cost of the presswork since preparation of the presses is required only at the beginning of a run.

In each department of the publishing house, a great deal of planning goes into the publication of a book, from the moment that the manuscript is ready. In the production department, it is necessary to set up schedules and maintain records—of when things should be done and when things are actually done. For sales and publicity purposes, dates on which proofs and finished books will be ready must be determined far in advance. Delays can be costly, can mean fewer sales, and can undermine carefully prepared publicity campaigns. Yet, with so many steps involved, and so many different suppliers and people involved, delays are sometimes difficult to avoid. The failure—and it can be a perfectly understandable one—of one person, one process, or one company along the line can cause a change in the entire schedule and

PRODUCTION SCHEDULE from Wackerow Date: 7-11-88

TO: Ed in Chief (Prashker) · Prod Editor (Schwarz) · Production (Hannon)
~~Potter (Salisbury)~~ · Publicity (Kahan) · Production (Otto) · 7/87
Harmony-(Guzzardi) · Advertising (Gray) · Production (Nicholas)
Editor (Allender) · Sch & Lib (Christiano) · Other (Sidrane) · [admin longsked]
Mg Editor (Stark) · Contracts (Shannon) · Compositor RPS
Copy Chief (Boorstein) · Art Director (grandits) · Printer Rae
Int. Sls. (Stevens) · ~~Designer~~ · Binder Horowitz
~~Art Sked Book (KS)~~

TITLE ALBERT & VICTORIA ISBN 570440 IMP 053

Trim Size 5 1/2" x 8 1/4" Text Pages 64 Insert — Qty 7500 @ $12.95

Mansucript to Compositor 7/1 · Repro from Comp 9/6

TEXT GGS
- To Production Editor 7/13
- Keyed gg to designer
- Dummy to Prod. Editor 7/27 (2wks)
- GG & Dummy to Prod/Des. 8/3 (1wk)
- GG release to Comp. 8/8 (3 dys)

MECHANICAL
- Materls to Mechanicaler —
- To Production/Designer 9/12 (4 dys)
- To Production Editor 9/12
- To Prod/Art for Correx 9/19 (1wk)
- Out to Printer 9/26 (1wk)

CAPT GG
- Ms to Compositor N.A.
- GG to Prod Ed/Designer
- Dummy to Prod. Editor
- GG & dummy to Prod/Designer
- All gg, contents, r/h to Comp

PRE PRESS
- /Blues to Prod 10/24
- Above checked & back to Ptr 10/28
- Sheets printed 11/18

PAGES
- To Prod. Editor 8/22 (2wks)
- Rev Dmy to Prod Editor —
- To Prod/Designer 8/29 (1wk)
- To Compositor 8/31 (2dys)

Bound books ready at bindery 12/16

Books in Avenel Pub Date

BOMS XX BLADS OTHER

INDEX
- Index Copy due Prod/Des. N.A.
- Ms to Compositor
- GG to Prod. Ed/Dusign
- GG to Compositor
- Repros Due
- PP/Mechs to Prod. Ed

EXT
- Flap/Cover copy due Prod on hand
- Jk/Cv Mech released by Oct. 1

INTERNATIONAL SALES: Prod. needs:
- Manuscript copy by
- Film Due By
- Mechanicals due by

Production schedule

consequently a delay of weeks or even months in the publication of a book.

In spite of possible delays, however, it is essential that a schedule be set up by the production supervisor and that every effort be made to keep to it. This schedule must take into consideration time for composition, proofreading of galleys, page makeup, reading of page proofs, preparation of an index, further corrections, platemaking, printing, binding, and shipping. In all, a publisher must plan on four to six months for the manufacture of a book. If a book is produced overseas, it will take an additional four to six weeks to ship it to the United States. There can be exceptions, jobs that can be rushed through in as short a time as a few weeks, if necessary, but these are costly and not common.

In addition to obtaining estimates, choosing suppliers, setting up schedules, and keeping track of each step of the book's production, the production supervisor is the person who will—sometimes with the help of the designer—choose the paper to be used. The selection of paper is a crucial one, since paper is not only important for the appearance of the book, but also represents a considerable percentage of the costs of making a book. Although the advice of the paper sales rep and the printer can be invaluable to the production supervisor when buying paper, it is most useful for the latter to bring a knowledge and understanding of the various qualities of paper to the job.

Several factors are involved in the selection of paper. Color is one. Although at a casual glance all paper might seem white, its range in color is actually considerable, from a pure white to a rather yellowish white.

Another factor is opacity, the amount of light that will show through from one side of the page to the other side.

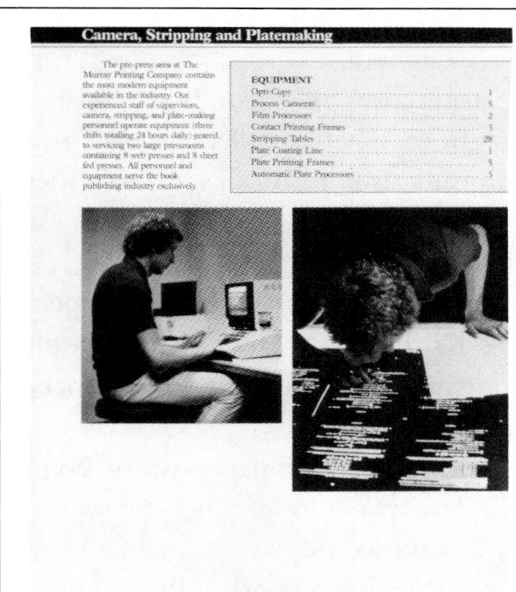

Camera, Stripping and Platemaking

The pre-press area at The Murray Printing Company contains the most modern equipment available in the industry. Our experienced staff of supervisors, camera, stripping, and plate-making personnel operate equipment (three shifts totalling 24 hours daily) geared to servicing two large pressrooms containing 8 web presses and 8 sheet fed presses. All personnel and equipment serve the book publishing industry exclusively.

EQUIPMENT	
Opti-Copy	1
Process Cameras	5
Film Processors	2
Contact Printing Frames	3
Stripping Tables	28
Plate Coating Line	1
Plate Printing Frames	5
Automatic Plate Processors	3

4

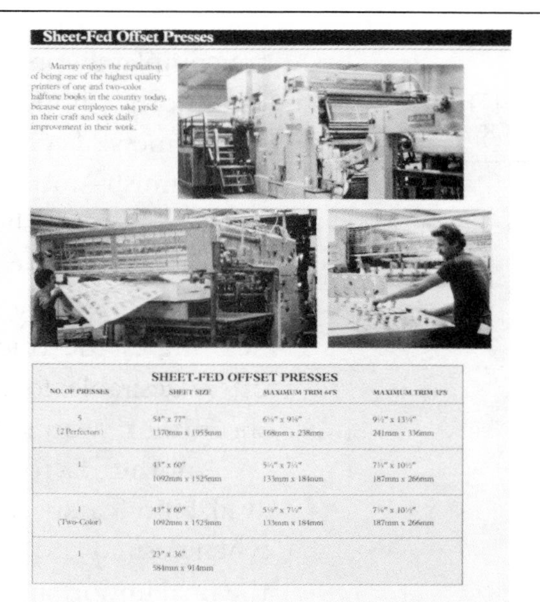

Sheet-Fed Offset Presses

Murray enjoys the reputation of being one of the highest quality printers of one and two-color halftone books in the country today, because our employees take pride in their craft and seek daily improvement in their work.

SHEET-FED OFFSET PRESSES

NO. OF PRESSES	SHEET SIZE	MAXIMUM TRIM 64'S	MAXIMUM TRIM 32'S
5 (2 Perfectors)	54" x 77" 1370mm x 1955mm	6⅝" x 9⅜" 168mm x 238mm	9½" x 13¼" 241mm x 336mm
1	43" x 60" 1092mm x 1525mm	5¼" x 7¼" 133mm x 184mm	7⅜" x 10½" 187mm x 266mm
1 (Two-Color)	43" x 60" 1092mm x 1525mm	5¼" x 7¼" 133mm x 184mm	7⅜" x 10½" 187mm x 266mm
1	23" x 36" 584mm x 914mm		

5

A printer's equipment list

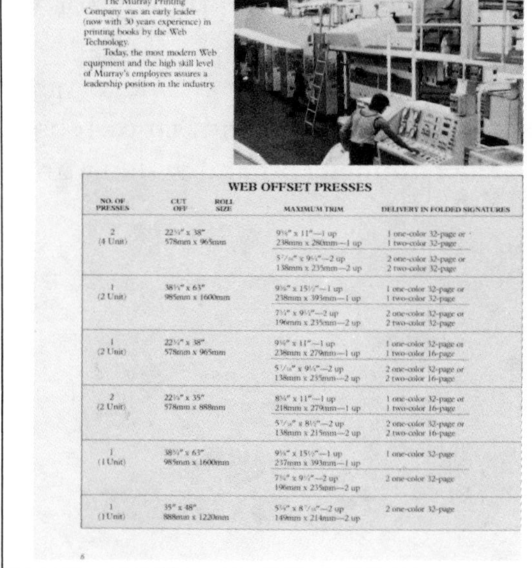

Web Presses

The Murray Printing Company was an early leader (now with 30 years experience) in printing books by the Web Technology.

Today, the most modern Web equipment and the high skill level of Murray's employees assures a leadership position in the industry.

WEB OFFSET PRESSES

NO. OF PRESSES	CUT OFF / ROLL SIZE	MAXIMUM TRIM	DELIVERY IN FOLDED SIGNATURES
2 (4 Unit)	22¾" x 38" 578mm x 965mm	9⅜" x 11"—1 up 238mm x 280mm—1 up	1 one-color 32-page or 1 two-color 32-page
		5⁷⁄₁₆" x 9¼"—2 up 138mm x 235mm—2 up	2 one-color 32-page or 2 two-color 32-page
1 (2 Unit)	38¾" x 63" 985mm x 1600mm	9⅜" x 15½"—1 up 238mm x 393mm—1 up	1 one-color 32-page or 1 two-color 32-page
		7¾" x 9¼"—2 up 196mm x 235mm—2 up	2 one-color 32-page or 2 two-color 32-page
1 (2 Unit)	22¾" x 38" 578mm x 965mm	9⅜" x 11"—1 up 238mm x 279mm—1 up	1 one-color 32-page or 1 two-color 16-page
		5⁷⁄₁₆" x 9¼"—2 up 138mm x 235mm—2 up	2 one-color 32-page or 2 two-color 16-page
2 (2 Unit)	22¾" x 35" 578mm x 888mm	8⅝" x 11"—1 up 218mm x 279mm—1 up	1 one-color 32-page or 1 two-color 16-page
		5⁷⁄₁₆" x 8½"—2 up 138mm x 215mm—2 up	2 one-color 32-page or 2 two-color 16-page
1 (1 Unit)	38¾" x 63" 985mm x 1600mm	9⅜" x 15½"—1 up 237mm x 393mm—1 up	1 one-color 32-page
		7¾" x 9¼"—2 up 196mm x 235mm—2 up	2 one-color 32-page
1 (1 Unit)	35" x 48" 888mm x 1220mm	5⅞" x 8⁷⁄₁₆"—2 up 149mm x 214mm—2 up	2 one-color 32-page

6

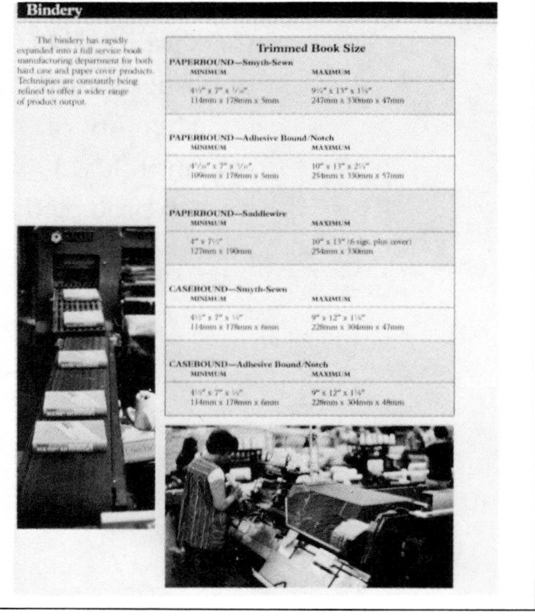

Bindery

The bindery has rapidly expanded into a full service book manufacturing department for both hard case and paper cover products. Techniques are constantly being refined to offer a wider range of product output.

Trimmed Book Size

	MINIMUM	MAXIMUM
PAPERBOUND—Smyth-Sewn	4½" x 7" x ³⁄₁₆" 114mm x 178mm x 5mm	9¾" x 13" x 1⅞" 247mm x 330mm x 47mm
PAPERBOUND—Adhesive Bound/Notch	4⁵⁄₁₆" x 7" x ³⁄₁₆" 109mm x 178mm x 5mm	10" x 13" x 2¼" 254mm x 330mm x 57mm
PAPERBOUND—Saddlewire	4" x 7½" 127mm x 190mm	10" x 13" (6 sigs. plus cover) 254mm x 330mm
CASEBOUND—Smyth-Sewn	4½" x 7" x ¼" 114mm x 178mm x 6mm	9" x 12" x 1⅞" 228mm x 304mm x 47mm
CASEBOUND—Adhesive Bound/Notch	4½" x 7" x ¼" 114mm x 178mm x 6mm	9" x 12" x 1⅞" 228mm x 304mm x 48mm

Some papers can be seen through rather easily, while others are completely opaque.

Another important distinction in paper is its finish, or smoothness. Papers vary from what is called rough, or antique, finish—most commonly used for books—to calendered or smooth, which is used for halftone illustrations, and coated, glossy paper, used for full-color books.

Bulk, too, is a consideration in the choice of paper. It determines the thickness of the book, and a thick book is often desirable for commercial reasons since it can make a short book seem longer than it actually is.

Another factor in the selection of paper is, of course, availability; a specific kind of paper might not be in stock when desired and a substitution would have to be made. And the final important factor in this choice is price. Prices of paper vary considerably, and the selection of paper might well depend on the overall budget for the book. Buying large quantities of paper at one time—for use in several books—can constitute a saving, and for this reason the production supervisor should take this into consideration in planning for the publisher's entire list.

The job of the production supervisor is one of great responsibility. Obviously, it is most important that each book be well produced for a predetermined cost and within a given period of time.

THE COMPOSITOR

The first step in the actual production of a book is composition, or typesetting—that is, the mechanical means of changing a typewritten manuscript into corresponding typefaces. Compositors use either metal type, which can be used directly for printing, or a photographic image, which is used to make printing plates. After nearly a century of little change, the years since the end of World War II have seen dramatic advancements in methods of composition, especially in the area of phototypesetting. Today, with the use of new computer technology, typesetting has become faster, easier, and cheaper, and even more revolutionary developments can be expected in the future.

In the past, the methods of book composition were basically two: cast metal, also known as hot type; and typewriter or direct impression, also referred to as cold type. The first of these methods includes hand composition and machine composition—Linotype or Intertype, and Monotype.

Pieces of metal type

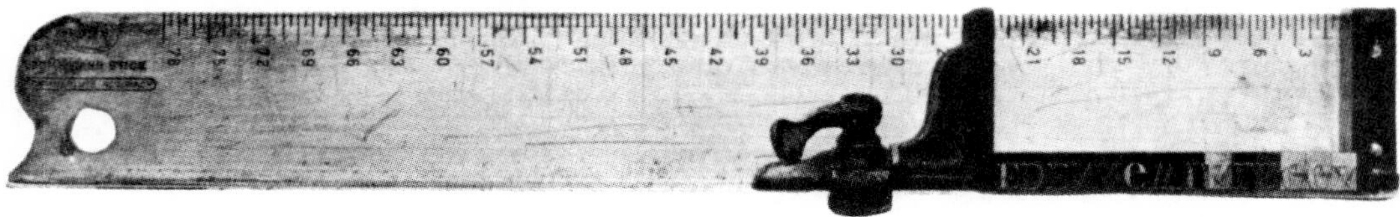

A composing stick

Type case

Compositor setting type

Hand composition has been used since the earliest days of bookmaking. It dates back to the time of Johann Gutenberg in 1450. Because it is both slow and costly, it is very rarely used for books today. Nonetheless, since many of the problems and principles involved apply to other, more commonly used methods, this method is worth describing.

The compositor takes the individual metal characters from a type case and puts them in a small metal tray, called a composing stick, which he holds in one hand. This stick is about ten picas deep (one pica is about one sixth of an inch) and has an adjustable bracket which controls the length of the line. Since the lines must be justified—that is, they must come out to an even length—thin pieces of metal of varying widths are placed between each word. When the stick is full, the type is transferred to an oblong metal tray, called a galley, where all the lines are assembled. Spacing between the lines is achieved by the insertion of metal strips, or slugs.

Machine composition was a later development; it was first used in the last part of the nineteenth century with the introduction of the Linotype machine. Linotype was the first and is still a widely used form of machine composition, although Intertype, practically identical to Linotype, is also frequently used.

The machine itself, though large and complex, has three basic parts: a typewriterlike keyboard; a magazine, in which the matrixes or molds of the letters are stored; and the caster. When the operator touches a key representing a letter, the matrix or mold slides down from the magazine and drops through a channel into position on the line being set. At the end of each word, a space bar is pushed, and a spaceband—an expandable steel wedge, thinner at the top than at the bottom—drops into place. When the line is nearly full, the

A Linotype machine

compositor pushes a bar that moves all the spacebands at once, thereby spreading the line as evenly as possible to the desired length. When the line is justified in this way, it is moved into the caster, where molten type metal is forced against it, filling in the incised areas, and a complete line of type, or slug, is produced and ejected onto the galley. The original matrixes are then returned to the channels from which they came so that they may be used again.

Monotype, the last system of cast-metal machine composition, was also developed in the latter part of the nineteenth century. This system makes use of two separate machines: a keyboard and a casting machine. The operator uses the keyboard as if it were a typewriter, but instead of producing readable copy, it produces, by means of compressed air, a roll of perforated ribbon—much like that used in a player piano. This roll, with its perforation, or code, is then placed on the machine, which follows its coded instruction, casting not a full line, like Linotype, but one character at a time. When the job is finished, every letter, number, punctuation mark, and space is on an individual piece of type. Because it is a high-quality, very expensive form of composition, Monotype is used almost exclusively for limited-edition books, collector's editions, and fine art books.

The second general method of composition, typewriter or direct impression (cold type), was developed in the middle of this century. The theory behind it is that of the ordinary typewriter. There is no casting of metal type, merely the striking of keys that impress, through high-quality carbon paper, an imprint of a character on a sheet of paper. A printing plate may be made by simply photographing that paper. However, the letter image and the spacing are of such low quality that it is seldom used in book publishing.

In recent years, the methods of composition described above have been rendered almost obsolete by the introduction of computer generated and assisted typography. Metal typesetting has been gradually replaced by phototypesetting and, increasingly, by digitized typesetting and other direct-image composition, which account for most of today's book typesetting.

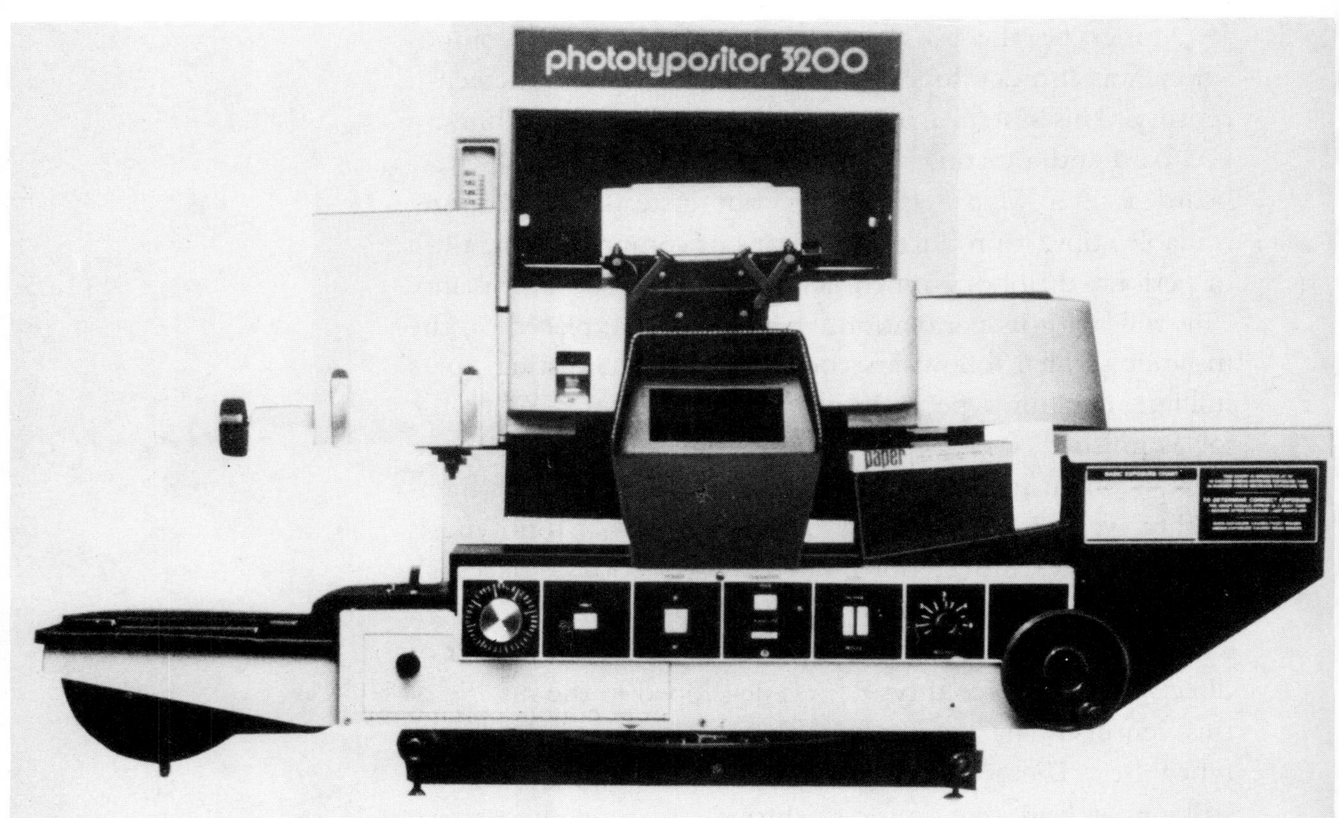

A Phototypositor machine used to set display type

As its name implies, phototypesetting is based on the principles of photography. The copy to be used in the making of the printing plates is created by exposing photosensitive paper or film to light formed into the shapes of type characters, and the paper or film is then processed like any other photograph. Phototypesetting is economical, capable of high-quality work, and timesaving—it reduces the number of production steps required for platemaking for every major printing process.

All phototypesetting requires three elements: a master character image, a light source, and the photosensitive material or film. Although phototypesetting systems have undergone three major evolutionary changes—defined by generation—all three generations begin with basically the same first step. An operator sits down at an input device, a typewriterlike keyboard, and copies the manuscript, also giving codes, stored in a computer, which dictate the type size, amount of space between letters, words, and lines, as well as the width of lines, justified or unjustified. The material is then put into the typesetter system, which creates the type images on the paper or film directly—by tape (paper or magnetic) or floppy disk.

The first generation of typesetters to produce photoset composition were merely adaptations of already existing machines. The Monophoto, Linofilm, and Fotosetter machines made use of the technology of the Monotype, Linotype, and Intertype machines, their matrixes containing a film negative of the character which was photographed rather than cast. Because these first-generation units were slow, due to the light sources used, they were soon replaced by units of the second generation, based on a new technology and electromechanical in nature.

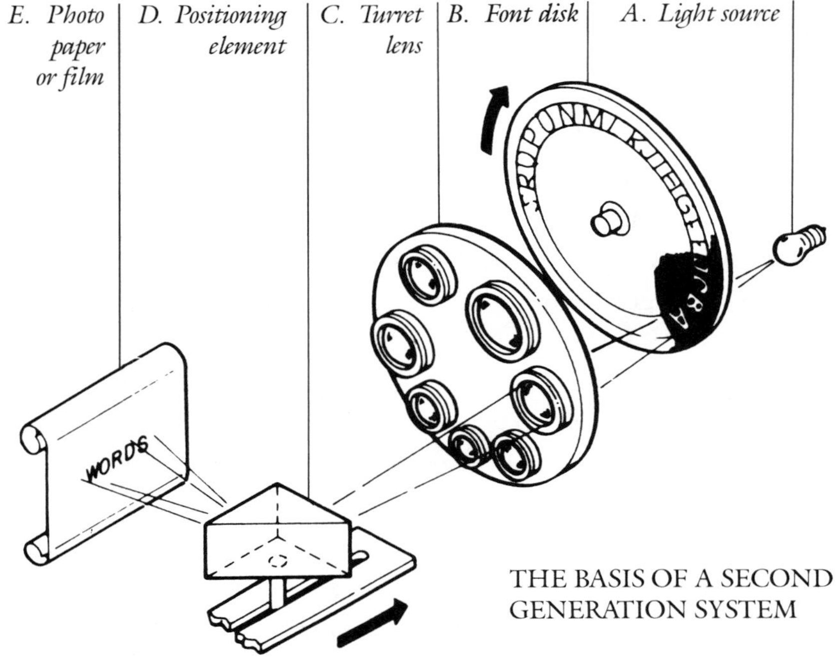

THE BASIS OF A SECOND GENERATION SYSTEM

The work of these second-generation units is shown in a simple drawing. Seen on the drawing, from right to left, are the light source (A), the font disk (B), the turret lens (C), the positioning element (D), and the photographic paper (E). The computer in the keyboard tells the light source and the font disk, a constantly rotating wheel, when they are lined up. Once lined up, the bulb at the light source flashes, and a brilliant beam of light passes through the negative of an individual character on the wheel. The light next passes through one of the lenses on the turret lens, causing the character to conform to the size instructed by the keyboard operator. The light then moves on to the positioning element, a mirror placed on a swivel so that the characters don't all flash on top of each other. The character then bounces off the mirror and flashes onto the photographic paper or film.

Third-generation phototypesetters differ from their predecessors in that they are entirely electronic; they utilize cathode ray tube (CRT) or laser technology. They employ information stored either as master images or in digital form to create images of characters, formed by a series of minute dots or lines, which are then transferred to photosensitive material. For this reason, the procedure is often referred to as digitized typesetting.

In many ways, the formation of character images in digitized typesetting is similar to the ways in which images are generated on a television screen, since, although these images, once printed, appear to be solid, accurately contoured shapes, they are actually patterns of characters and consist of sweeps of scan lines and dots. The density of the scan lines determines

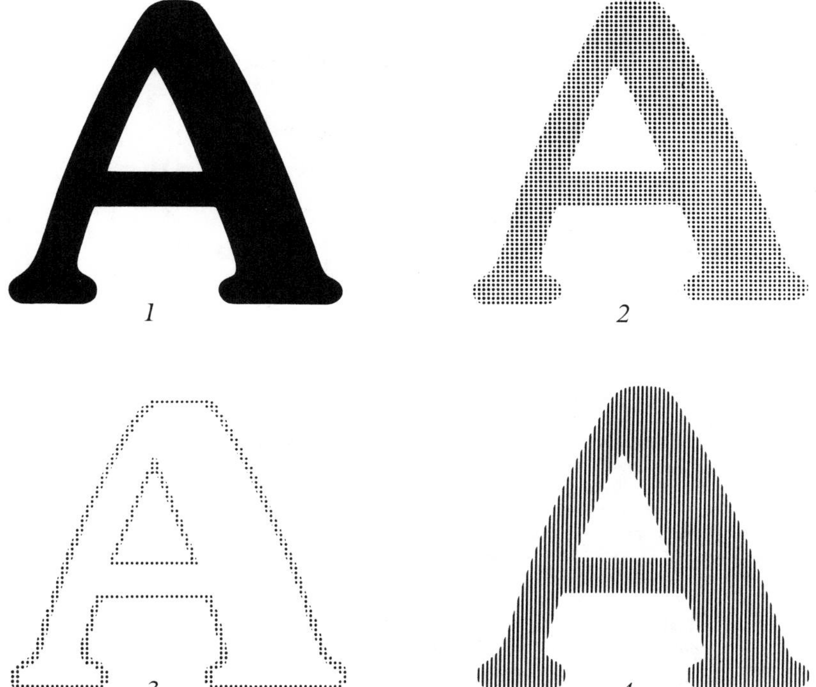

Computer generated digitized type. 1. Original drawing of the letter. 2. The computer maps the letter by electronically scanning the original and turning it into digital codes called pixels. 3. The outline of the letter is refined. 4. The computer's cathode ray tube paints in between the points to create the letter. There are 1950 vertical strokes per inch.

Chapter 2
Football on Madden's Lot: Field Goals Were Never Big

All sports involve the same basic skills: hand-eye coordination, balance, concentration, positioning your body. But team sports can teach you an important skill for life: how to get along with people.

As part of a team, you always have to be thinking about your teammates. You can't just do your own thing. That's a term I always hated: "do your own thing." People don't get many chances to run around "doing their own thing." Mostly you have to do the best job you can within a group, whether it's school, society, or a team.

Individual sports can help you be a great athlete. They can teach you how to do your best. But if you only play individual sports, you're missing out on the friendships a team sport can give you.

When you're young, there's really no need to choose between sports to play. The best athletes are the ones who are good at everything. You should play basketball, football, soccer, stickball, tennis, baseball, anything you can. Actually, I've always thought that your favorite sport should be whatever's in season.

If you only want to play football, and it's March, there won't be anyone to play with. Everyone will be playing baseball and basketball. If you want to play baseball in November, it's hard to get up a game.

I know because I was the kid who got the guys together.

I grew up near San Francisco, in Daly City, California. There was a small empty lot next to our house that everyone called Madden's Lot. I thought the place belonged to me. I found out that it didn't when somebody started building a house there. But until then, that's where my friends and I had games. And since it was my lot, I had to figure out how football was played.

So I went to Kezar Stadium, where the 49ers and the University of San Francisco played football, and just looked at things: where they put the yard markers, the boundaries, and how many points they got for what. Then I came back and we did it ourselves.

We'd play all kinds of football on the lot—touch, tac-kle, sometimes just short-yardage games. Put the ball near the goal line and see if you could score.

Nobody was telling us what to do because they didn't have organized youth leagues back then. There wasn't such a thing as Pop Warner, and I'm glad there wasn't.

Learning how to play football means learning how to organize, learning how to get together, learning how to lead. When everything's organized for you, the leadership is coming from adults. Leadership should be coming from you.

A galley

the typographic quality of the imaged characters; the more scan lines to the inch, the greater the sharpness of the characters, which may also be electronically obliqued, back-slanted, condensed, expanded, or reversed.

There are many advantages to these third-generation phototypesetters. For one, they are capable of extremely high speeds. Furthermore, since patterns of the needed characters are called out of the memory section of an on-line device or from paper or magnetic tapes and are imaged in the precise size and at the precise position on the page, they can create complete pages of text, headline, and graphics material, eliminating many steps required in earlier systems.

There will undoubtedly be further advances in the methods of composition, and new generations of phototypesetters, but once type has been set, by whatever means, it will always be necessary to check the accuracy of the composition, to make certain that the compositor has followed the author's copy, along with the editor's changes and the designer's instructions. For this purpose, it is necessary to make—or pull—proofs. These are called galley proofs (the type in Linotype or Monotype composition was kept in a tray called a galley) even when no galleys are involved. In the case of hot-metal composition, these proofs are pulled on a small letterpress; cold type or phototype are photocopied.

The compositor's proofs, together with the original manuscript, are sent to the publishing house for further proofreading; this work will be described in the next chapter. They are then returned to the compositor, who makes the necessary corrections and then divides the type in the galleys into pages. The designer's layout is the guide to the length of the page as well as to the insertion of special type matter such as running heads, page numbers, chapter heads, and subheads.

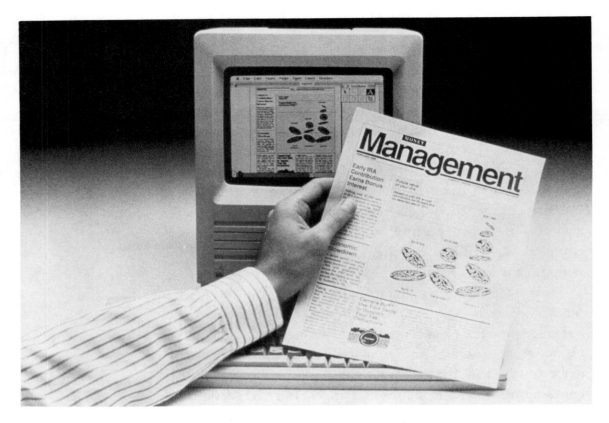

The Apple Mac SE20 can make pages with headlines in position

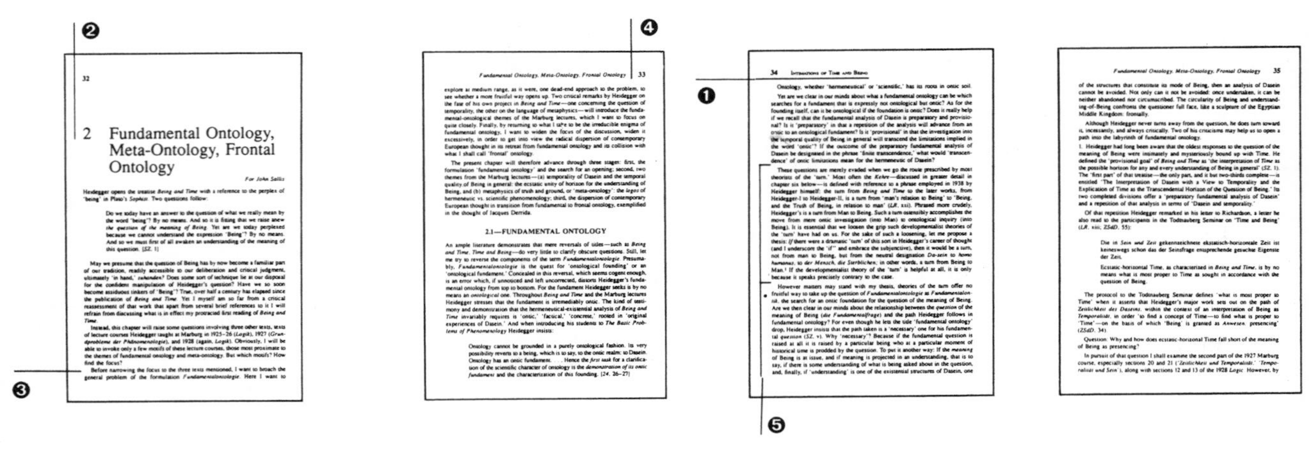

32

2 Fundamental Ontology, Meta-Ontology, Frontal Ontology

For John Sallis

Fundamental Ontology, Meta-Ontology, Frontal Ontology 33

2.1—FUNDAMENTAL ONTOLOGY

34 INTIMATIONS OF TIME AND BEING

Fundamental Ontology, Meta-Ontology, Frontal Ontology 35

MagnaPage automatically makes pages with 1. running heads in position 2. chapter titles in position 3. widows and orphans controlled 4. pages numbered automatically 5. space increased or decreased to make pages align

The proofs—called page proofs—are corrected by the compositor as well as by the publisher's proofreader. They are then returned to the compositor—sometimes accompanied by an index, which the compositor will set and which will have to be checked and corrected as was the main text of the manuscript.

With electronic, third-generation typesetting, the copy can be set directly into pages, eliminating the galley stage. In this case, the two sets of proofs that are pulled and sent to the publisher for checking may be called paged galleys and pages, or first and second pass.

THE PROOFREADER AND THE INDEXER

The set of proofs which has been corrected by the printer's proofreader is called the master set and is sent to the publishing house, along with at least two other sets. The master set will be read by the publisher's proofreader, who checks it carefully against the manuscript. In addition, the proofreader checks for printer's mistakes in spelling and punctuation, dropped or repeated material, as well as the correctness of word division, or hyphenation, at the end of lines. The proofreader's responsibility is great, and a failure to correct errors can ruin all the good work that has been done on the original manuscript. Furthermore, the publisher's proofreader must carefully examine typographic quality—damaged or broken letters, and characters of the wrong font or wrong point size that may have been mistakenly set.

Typographic quality is also checked by the designer, who receives a set of galleys, but the designer's main concern is to see that all design instructions have been followed. Typeface and size, length of lines, word spacing and letter spacing—these are the things that must be examined most carefully. Minute attention, too, must be paid to any special matter and display faces used in the book and to any complicated layout.

Finally, a set of galleys is sent to the author, who reads them for errors, keeping in mind that this is most probably the last chance to make corrections that could improve the book. These corrections can be in the form of deletions, additions, changes in sentence structure, and so on. New facts might have come to light between the time the book was written and the manuscript was set into type, and these might entail rather extensive revisions, just as a sentence that seemed just right when first written might seem awkward a few months later. Authors are told not to rewrite their books in galleys. They are told that extensive changes are time-consuming and could delay publication of the book by upsetting a carefully planned schedule, sometimes even making it necessary for a compositor to supply a set of revised galleys, and that changes are expensive to make and could cost the author a considerable amount of money. Changes in galleys are carefully distinguished between printer's errors (marked PE after each change), author's alterations (marked AA after each change), and editorial alterations (marked EA after each change). Although the printer is responsible for the PEs, it is the publisher who pays for the AAs and EAs, and generally a publisher, by contract, will pay no more than a sum equivalent to 10 percent of the original composition bill, charging the author for anything above this amount.

When all changes and corrections have been made on the various sets of galleys, they are coordinated and transferred to the master set which is returned, together with the manuscript, to the compositor. Proofreaders' correction marks are

OPERATIONAL SIGNS

ẟ	Delete
⁀	Close up; delete space
(ẟ)	Delete and close up
#	Insert space
eq #	Make space between words equal; make leading between lines equal
hr #	Insert hair space
ls	Letterspace
¶	Begin new paragraph
no ¶	Run paragraphs together
□	Move type one em from left or right
⊐	Move right
⊏	Move left
][	Center
⊓	Move up
⊔	Move down
=	Straighten type; align horizontally
||	Align vertically
tr	Transpose
(sp)	Spell out
stet	Let it stand
⊥	Push down type; check type image

TYPOGRAPHICAL SIGNS

lc	Lowercase capital letter
cap	Capitalize lowercase letter
sc	Set in small capitals
ital	Set in italic type
rom	Set in roman type
bf	Set in boldface type
wf	Wrong font; set in correct type
×	Reset broken letter; check repro or film
9	Reverse (type upside down)

PUNCTUATION MARKS

^	Insert comma
∨	Insert apostrophe (or single quotation mark)
“ ”	Insert quotation marks
⊙	Insert period
(set) ?	Insert question mark
;)	Insert semicolon
:(	Insert colon
|=|	Insert hyphen
1/M	Insert em dash
1/N	Insert en dash

Proofreaders' marks

Authors As Proofreaders

"I don't care what kind of type you use for my book," said a myopic author to the publisher, but please print the galley proofs in large type. Perhaps in the future such a request will not sound so ridiculous to those familar with the printing process. today, however, type once set is not reset exepct to correct errors.[1]

1. Type may be reduced in size, or enlarged photographically when a book is printed by offset.

Proofreading is an Art and a craft. All authors should know the rudiiments thereof though no proofreader expects them to be masters of it. Watch proofreader expects them to be masters of it. Watch not only for misspelled or incorrect works (often a most illusive error but also for misplace dspaces, "unclosde" quotation marks and parenthesis, and imporper paragraphing; and learn to recognize the difference between an em dash—used to separate an interjectional part of a sentence—and an en dash used commonly between continuing numbers (e.g., pp. 5–10; A.d. 1165-70) and the word dividing hyphen. Sometimes, too, a letter from a wrong font will creep a mathematical forumla. Whatever is *underlined* in into the printed text, or a boldface **k** or d turn up in a MS. should of course, be italicized in print. To find the errors overlooked by the proofreader is the authors first problem in proof reading. The second problem is to make corrections using the marks and symbols, devized by proffessional proofreaders, that any trained typesetter will understand. The third—and most difficult problem for authors proofreading their own works is to resist the temptation to rewrite in proofs.

Manuscript editor

A marked-up galley

PAGE
PROOF
PAGE - 4

86 John Madden

Toughness

Toughness isn't a macho thing. The great fullback Larry Csonka once defined toughness for me. "Toughness," he said, "is the ability to do everything with the same enthusiasm, including things you don't enjoy."

At the time, Zonk was one of the great first-and-ten players of all time. Everytime he got the ball on first and ten, he'd run it up the middle and people would start piling on his shoulders, his thighs, his legs, his ankles, and finally bring Zonk down. He'd gain eight yards with eleven guys on him.

Nobody enjoys getting hit like that, but it was the job Csonka had to do, and he did it with enthusiasm.

Aggressiveness

Great players win games by making things happen.

I'll never forget a play my Raider cornerback, Willie Brown, made late in 1973. We were playing in Houston, and we were ahead. An Oiler receiver caught a pass across the field, but Willie chased him anyway and hauled him down on the 2-yard line. On the next play, the Oilers fumbled; Phil Villapiano recovered and ran the ball back fifty-two yards. We ended up winning, 17–6, but if Willie hadn't hauled down that receiver, we might have lost.

The really important thing about Willie's play was that he was so far away from the ball, if he hadn't chased the receiver, I wouldn't have noticed. My assistant coaches wouldn't have noticed. But Willie was aggressive, he made something happen. Willie didn't have to chase the receiver, but he did—and caught him.

The First Book of Football

Pride

Great players have a commitment to be the best and a fear that they might *not* be. That fear of failure motivates them. Without pride, fear of failure is just fear.

In the locker room before a Pro Bowl game, I noticed that O.J. Simpson just couldn't sit still. This wasn't O.J. Simpson the actor and television commercial star. This was the O.J. who had rushed for a record 2,003 yards that season.

I said to him, "Is this game that big to you?"

"Every game is that big," O.J. said. "I don't want to be *one* of the best. I want to be the *best* of the best."

"That's why you are the best of the best," I said.

Knowledge

A player has to not only know how to play his own position, but how all the players on the team play theirs. Any time a tackle says to me, "I'm the tackle, I don't know what the guard does," I'm not impressed. If the tackle doesn't know what the guard does, then he can't really know his *own* job either.

Dedication

Willingness to work. When a great player messes up a play, he'll work until he gets it right. An average player won't. That's why he's average.

Any of these are qualities great players share. How did they get them?

From playing the game.

Page proofs

standard symbols, which clearly indicate to the compositor what changes should be made. It is essential that all proofreaders know these symbols, and it is most useful if authors, too, are familiar with them.

After the galleys have been corrected and divided into pages by the compositor, page proofs are sent to the publishing house, where they are carefully examined to see if the galley corrections have been followed. At this time, corrected areas are reread to see that new errors have not been made while old ones were being corrected. Top and bottom lines of each page are also checked to make sure that no lines have been dropped during the division into pages. (The designer again checks to see that all instructions have been followed.)

Further editorial work is done at this point, since all the pages have been given numbers. This means that cross-references, table of contents, and lists of illustrations can be completed by the insertion of accurate page numbers. It also means that an index can be prepared.

The indexer's job is one requiring patience, skill, and accuracy. Before the actual work can begin, the indexer must know just what kind of index is required. There are several possibilities: A name index means that only names of people will be listed; a proper noun index would involve names of places, works of art or literature, and names of organizations as well as people. Most difficult of all is an index which includes concepts—censorship, colonialism, or poetry, to give a few examples—and which often calls for subentries as well as main entries.

Indexers have different methods of working, but in general they first read through the proofs quickly to get an idea of the nature of the work and the problems that may arise. Next, the proofs are very carefully read, and those words to be included in the index are underlined while concepts will be noted in the margins. After that, indexers transfer the underlined words

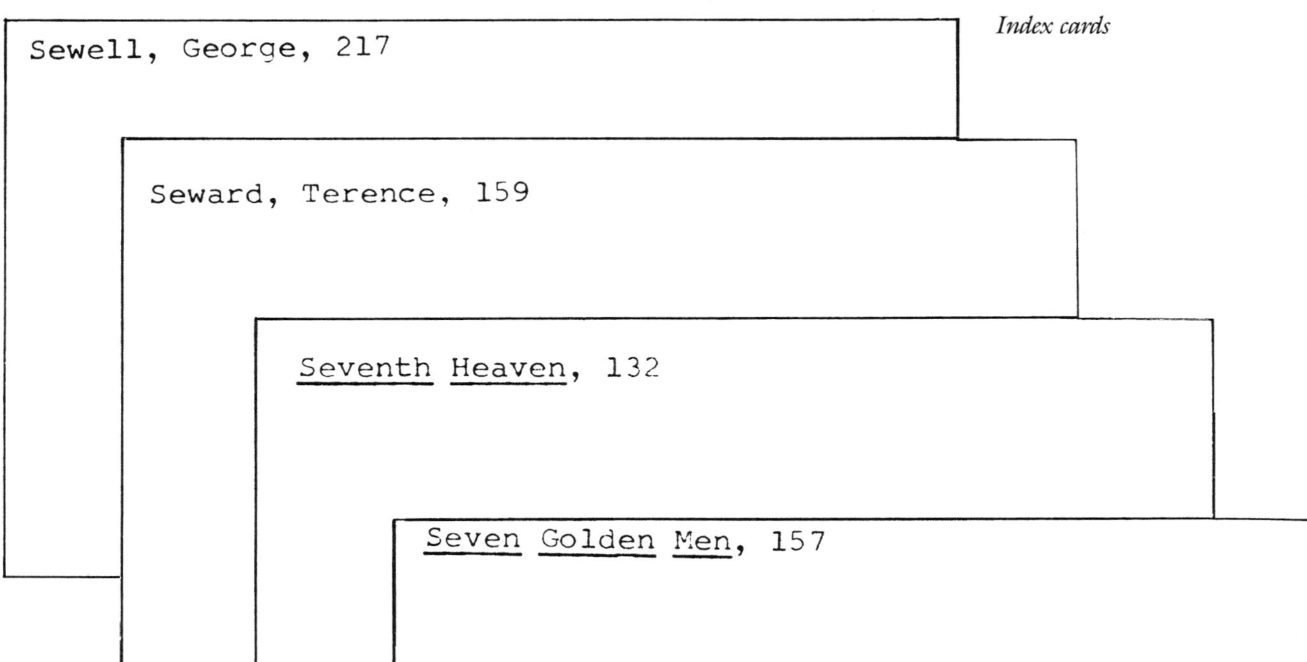

Index cards

Aiken, Conrad, 8

Aldington, Richard, 85, 123,

124

Anderson, Margaret, 81, 119, 131

Anderson, Sherwood, 43-46, 48,

51, 59, 60, 63, 72, 152

Dark Laughter, 59

Winesburg, Ohio, 46

Ansermet, Ernest, 98, 99, 100,

114

Antheil, George, 23, 101-103,

105-110, 115, 153, 160, 162

Ballet Méchanique, 108-110

Symphony in F, 108

Apollinaire, Guillaume, 23

Aragon, Louis, 13

Auric, Georges, 98

Baker, Josephine, 158

Balanchine, George, 93

Barnes, Djuna, 72, 133

Set index:
2 columns (12 × 1 × 12 picas)
10/13 Bodoni reg., c/lc
× 12 picas
flush left, ragged right.
Indent sub-entries 1/M,
runovers 2 ems.
first page 34 ll per col.
full pp. 68 ll. per col.

An index ready for typesetting

and noted concepts to individual 3 × 5 file cards (some may use electronic cards and computers) which also carry the corresponding page numbers. These cards are then coordinated and alphabetized; some compositors will agree to set the index from these cards, while others require that the index be typed as any other copy would be.

Many word-processing software packages have index capabilities that can be an aid to the indexer. But the difficult job of organizing and making sure everything makes sense can only be done by a human.

The index is an important part of a book and can be of enormous value to the reader. Because of this, it is essential that it be accurately prepared to direct the reader to the correct page and painstakingly corrected once it has been composed. Some indexes are so difficult and complex that the indexer will—with good reason—be given credit in the book for his or her work.

THE PRINTER

The printer's job is, of course, an essential one, since everything so far has led toward the transformation of the author's manuscript into a book and this can be achieved only by printing. It is the printer's responsibility to prepare plates that will carry the images (both type and art) of the contents of the book. It is then the printer's responsibility to print the book—that is, to transfer these images to large sheets of paper, which will be folded and bound into finished books. Machines now do much of the work that was once done by man, but the printer controls those machines and must have a thorough knowledge of their functions and how they can best be utilized.

There are several different methods by which books can be printed, each requiring a different kind of plate; the most commonly used today is called photo offset lithography or, more simply, offset. The principle of this way of printing is the natural antipathy of grease and water. It is known as *photo*

A fifteenth-century printer

offset because the printing plates are prepared with the use of photo emulsions.

The printer makes these films from the mechanicals that have been supplied by the designer. These mechanicals are mounted on a camera board and are photographed to obtain a negative film. The negative is developed and carefully examined for every detail; it is then positioned and taped onto a sheet of goldenrod, an opaque orange-yellow paper that serves as a support. This procedure is called stripping. When everything is firmly in place, the stripper cuts windows in the goldenrod paper where it covers the image areas so that light can pass through them during exposure to the plate. The result of this work is called a flat, which is the same size as the press sheet.

Proofing of these flats is generally done on blueprint paper. The blueprints are made by exposing a chemically treated

STAGES OF THE PRINTING PROCESS

1. Mechanical ready to be shot by camera

2. Negatives are developed

3. Negatives are stripped onto goldenrod flats

4. Flat is shot for press plates

5. Plates are on press

6. Final press sheets

paper, together with a flat, to a strong arc light in a vacuum printing frame. When developed in a liquid bath, the result is a contact print or a positive proof, from which it is possible for the designer to tell if the assembled image elements have been properly positioned and if there are any defects in the flat.

The actual making of offset plates is a complex process, the aim being to produce a thin sheet of metal with printing and nonprinting areas based on the principle that grease and water do not mix. Since these areas are almost level, chemical means must be employed to see that the printing areas will be water repellent, and that the nonprinting areas will be ink repellent.

Many different kinds of offset plates are made, but they can be divided into two categories: The first, and by far the most commonly used, are known as additive plates. A metal sheet is coated with an emulsion, a light-sensitive, ink-receptive substance. When the plate is exposed to light through the negative film, the coating hardens and becomes insoluble in the printing areas, while remaining soft in the nonprinting areas. A water-receptive material that attaches itself only to the uncoated metal is then applied. In this way, the plate is divided into printing and nonprinting parts. Additive plates are relatively inexpensive. Their main disadvantage is environmental; many harsh chemicals are used, and disposing of these chemicals is potentially dangerous.

The second type of offset plate, known as subtractive plates, most probably constitutes the wave of the future. Chemicals are already on these plates—they don't have to be added, and because of this there is almost no harmful residue. These plates, which are developed in water after having been exposed to light, can be used for far longer runs than can additive plates. Their major disadvantage is their cost, which is five times greater than that of other plates.

Once the plates have been made, actual printing can begin. Printing presses are complicated machines that must perform several functions. They must be capable of holding the plate firmly in position. They must be able to provide for the application of the ink essential to printing. Each press, too, must have a device for the exact placement of the paper on which the image will be printed. There must be a means of applying the pressure to print that image, and there must be a way for printed sheets to be removed as well as a place for them to be temporarily stored. In addition, each press must have room to hold blank paper and ink preparatory to use. Thus, a printing press performs many functions, either simultaneously or in a carefully planned sequence.

Presses used for offset printing are called rotary presses; they function by means of a series of cylinders. The plates with their grease-receptive printing areas and water-receptive non-printing areas are clamped to a plate cylinder. This cylinder rotates and comes into contact first with rollers wet by water or another dampening solution, and then with rollers wet

SIDE VIEW OF OFFSET PRINTING CYLINDERS

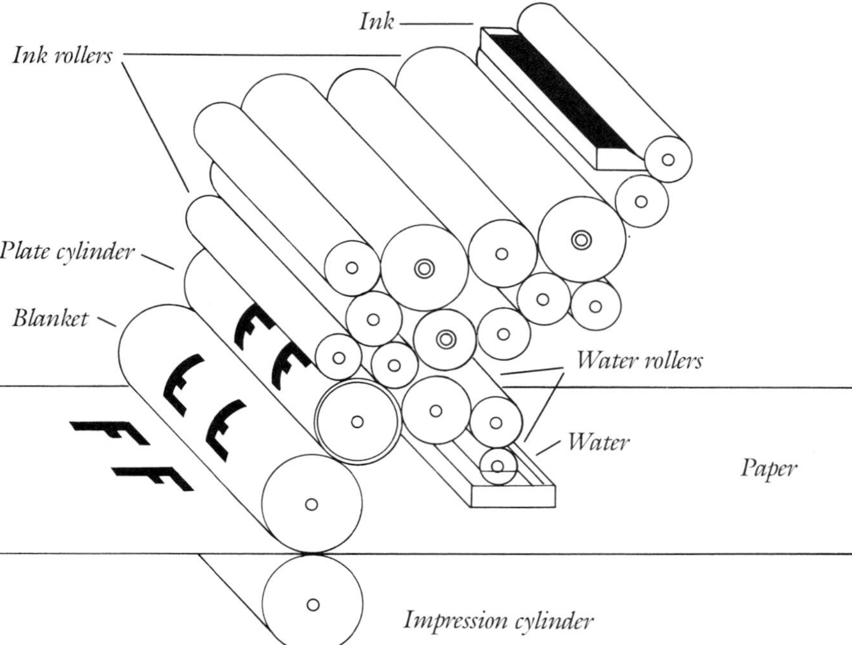

Offset printing cylinders

with ink. The water prevents the oily ink from wetting the nonprinting areas.

The printing areas, now inked, rotate on their cylinder against another cylinder which carries a rubber blanket. The inked image is thus transferred, or offset, onto this blanket cylinder.

The blanket cylinder, in turn, rotates against an impression cylinder. Paper, which has been lifted from a feed pile by suction and blowers, passes between the turning blanket and impression cylinders, picking up the image from the blanket before being moved to a delivery pile.

A second method of printing is letterpress, which was until recently the most widely used way of printing a book. It can be described as printing from raised surfaces which are inked and then pressed against paper on which they leave an impression. An ordinary rubber stamp is a simple example of this.

There are many kinds of plates or image carriers—metal, plastic, rubber, magnesium, and others—which are suitable for letterpress printing, all based on the principle of a mold which can be taken from type and illustrations and converted into permanent plates. Printing—except from metal type, which cannot be curved—is usually carried out on a rotary press.

The letterpress process most widely used in the production of books today is the Cameron Belt Press. It represents a major breakthrough in that it prints a complete book in one step. The plates for half the book are mounted on one belt and the plates for the second half are mounted on a second belt. Each belt is a continuous loop, and each loop is a printing unit. Paper from a roll is fed first into one printing unit and then into the other. When the printing is completed, the paper is cut, and the pages collated and bound.

Another method of printing, not widely used for books in the United States, is gravure. It is especially effective for the printing of photographs or other illustrations reproduced by

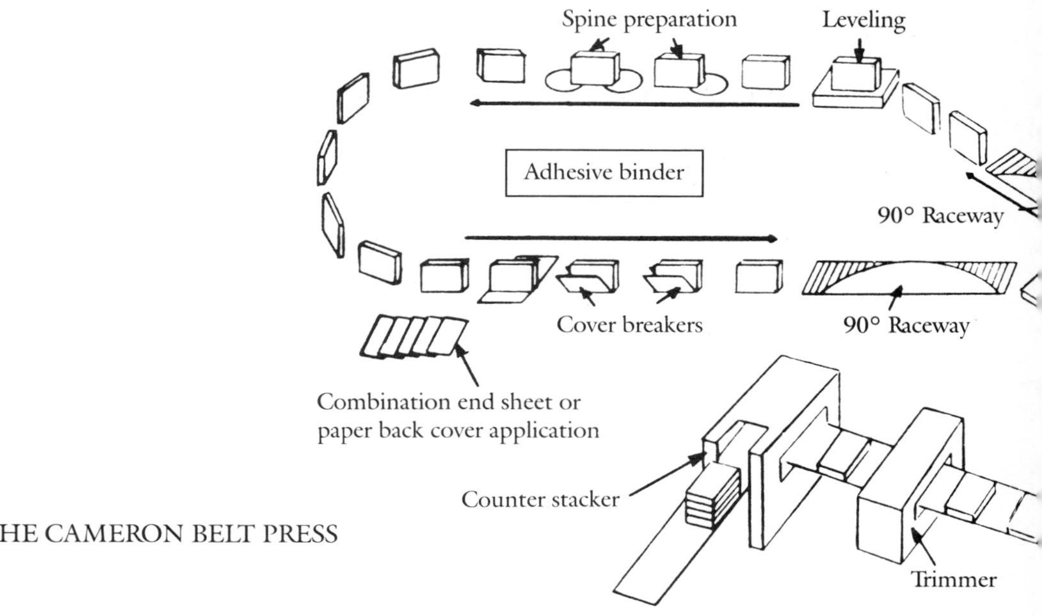

THE CAMERON BELT PRESS

means of halftones, or patterns of dots. Gravure, however, reproduces type less effectively and is extremely expensive. Whereas offset printing prints from almost completely flat surfaces and letterpress from raised surfaces, gravure is printed from sunken or depressed surfaces. The lines that are to print are cut below the surface of the plates.

Whatever way of printing is used—offset, letterpress, or gravure—once the printer has completed his work, the manuscript is well on its way to becoming a book. Before it can be called that, however, the large printed sheets provided by the printer must be folded, assembled in the proper sequence (gathered), and bound. Before describing this final step in the production of a book, it is best to examine the special problems involved in color printing.

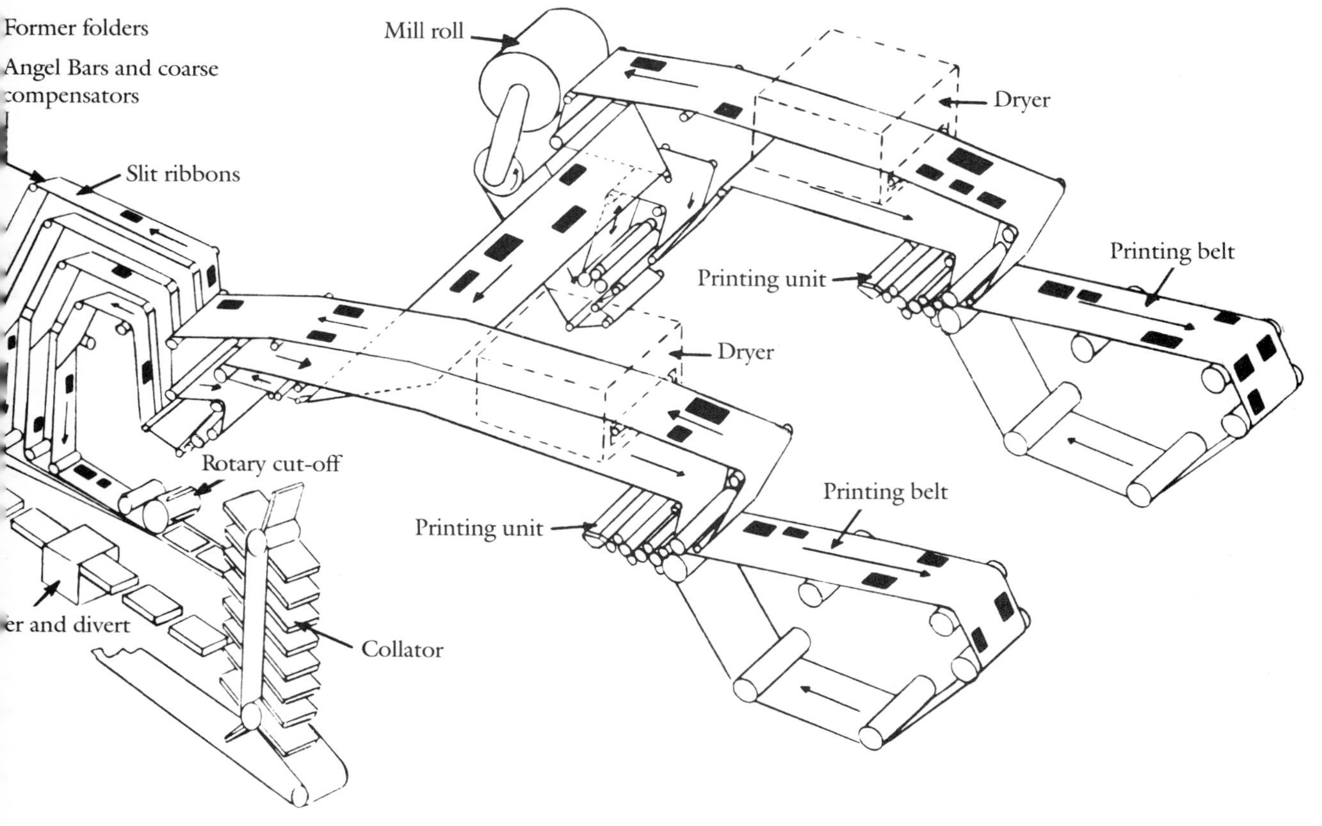

THE COLOR PRINTER

Most books are printed in one color, and that color is black. However, several kinds of books call for more than one color, and the printing of these books is both more costly and more complicated than the black-and-white printing already discussed.

Although an extra color or extra colors can be used for merely decorative purposes, to enrich the appearance of a book, there are many cases in which color printing is essential. Some textbooks, for example, include charts and graphs that become clearer in meaning with the use of color. Maps often require color printing, and an added color can be helpful in distinguishing one kind of text block from another. Children find colors attractive, and for this reason a large number of children's books are illustrated in color. Art books require color printing for the reproduction of paintings in which color plays an important part, and reproductions of color photographs enhance the value—both commercial and esthetic—of a gift book. In a world in which we are accustomed to seeing images in color rather than in black and white, the use of color illustrations in books, too, is increasing.

The reason for the high cost of color printing can be easily understood; after all, it takes four times as much work to print four colors as it does to print one color. And the complexity of color printing can best be illustrated by an explanation of the two kinds of color printing. The first of these, known as full color or process color, is the more complex of the two. Because it can yield a very wide range of colors, it is used for the reproduction of paintings, color photographs, and other subjects which require a large number of colors for faithful reproduction.

There are two kinds of copy used for full-color printing: the original work of art itself, or a color photographic slide—often called a transparency—of the original. In order to make plates for full-color reproduction, the colors of the copy must first be separated by a camera or an electronic scanner into each primary color.

To do this, the copy is photographed at least three times with a special lens. One lens is covered with a red filter, the second lens with a green filter, and the third with a blue filter. The red filter produces a negative of all the red light, which is called a red separation negative; the green filter produces a green separation negative; and the blue filter, a blue separation negative. A positive is then made of each negative. The red one produces a combination of blue and green, which is called cyan; the green produces a combination of red and blue, called magenta; and the blue produces a combination of red and green, which is yellow. These are the three colors of what are called the process inks, those which combine to bring the widest possible range of colors, and are thus used in full-color printing. In most cases, in addition to these three separations, a black separation will be made to add depth and brilliance to the reproduction; this is obtained by placing a red, green, and blue filter successively before the lens while the copy is photographed.

Ideally, these separations should result in a perfectly faithful reproduction of the copy, but due to imperfections in printing inks and paper, they do not, so that a great deal of correction of the negative is necessary. This is done manually, photographically, or, in recent times, electronically.

Hand correction is a very complicated task, performed by specialists who closely examine the negatives, eliminate the flaws in the film, and opaque and retouch when necessary. By dot-etching, they are able to reduce or increase the size or number of halftone dots with the use of chemicals.

Photographically, corrections can be made by masking. In this procedure, a set of separation negatives is made with special filters. These are combined with the primary set, and serve to control the density, modifying or eliminating unwanted colors.

Today, manual and photographic correction can be eliminated by the use of electronic color scanners, which both separate and balance the colors.

Plates for full-color printing are made photomechanically. The corrected negatives are exposed against sensitized film to make positives. The positives are then placed against another film with a halftone screen in between them. The resultant screened halftone negatives are used to make the plates. Since the colored dots generally print alongside each other, the halftone screens are usually placed at different angles for each color.

The proofs from which the printer can check and control color work are called progressives. Each of the colors used is shown singly and in combination. There will be a yellow proof and a magenta proof; then a proof of yellow and magenta together. Then there will be a cyan proof, followed by a yellow, magenta, and cyan proof. Then a black proof will be made, followed by a proof of all four colors together.

Preparation and correction of these progressives is a costly and painstaking job, as well as a crucial one. Each color plate is minutely examined, as are the color combination and the register, or exact alignment, of the plates. With today's technology and skills, good full-color printing can come close to the original work, but only if it is carefully planned, prepared, and controlled.

The second kind of color printing is known as multicolor or flat color. For flat-color printing, the printer will generally be provided with mechanicals for the entire book. These mechanicals consist of the art, which may or may not have been preseparated by the illustrator (see the chapter on the illustrator), combined with the text, which has been positioned and pasted in by the designer of the book.

When, as is generally the case, the colors have not been preseparated by the illustrator and have to be camera-separated by the printer, all the art is placed on one board, with no overlays. It is photographed several times in black and white, one time for each color to be used. Each negative is then opaqued—that is, the areas not wanted as part of the plate are painted out, so that each negative before platemaking will contain only those parts to be printed in any given color.

Platemaking for flat-color printing is the same as for black-and-white printing. However, a separate plate will be made for

PRIMARY LIGHT COLORS

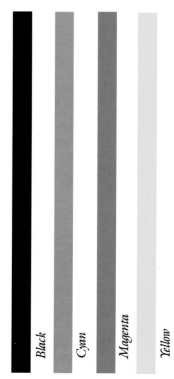

PRINTING PROCESS COLORS

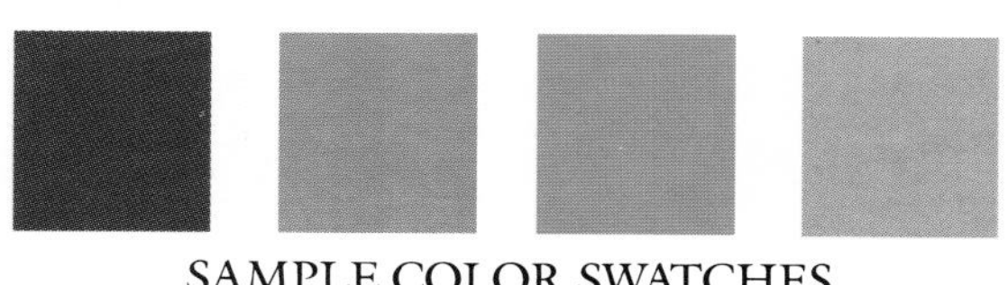
SAMPLE COLOR SWATCHES

Magenta

Yellow

Magenta and yellow

Cyan

Cyan and yellow

Cyan, yellow, and magenta

Black

Magenta, yellow, cyan, and black

A variety of percentage mixes of the four process colors

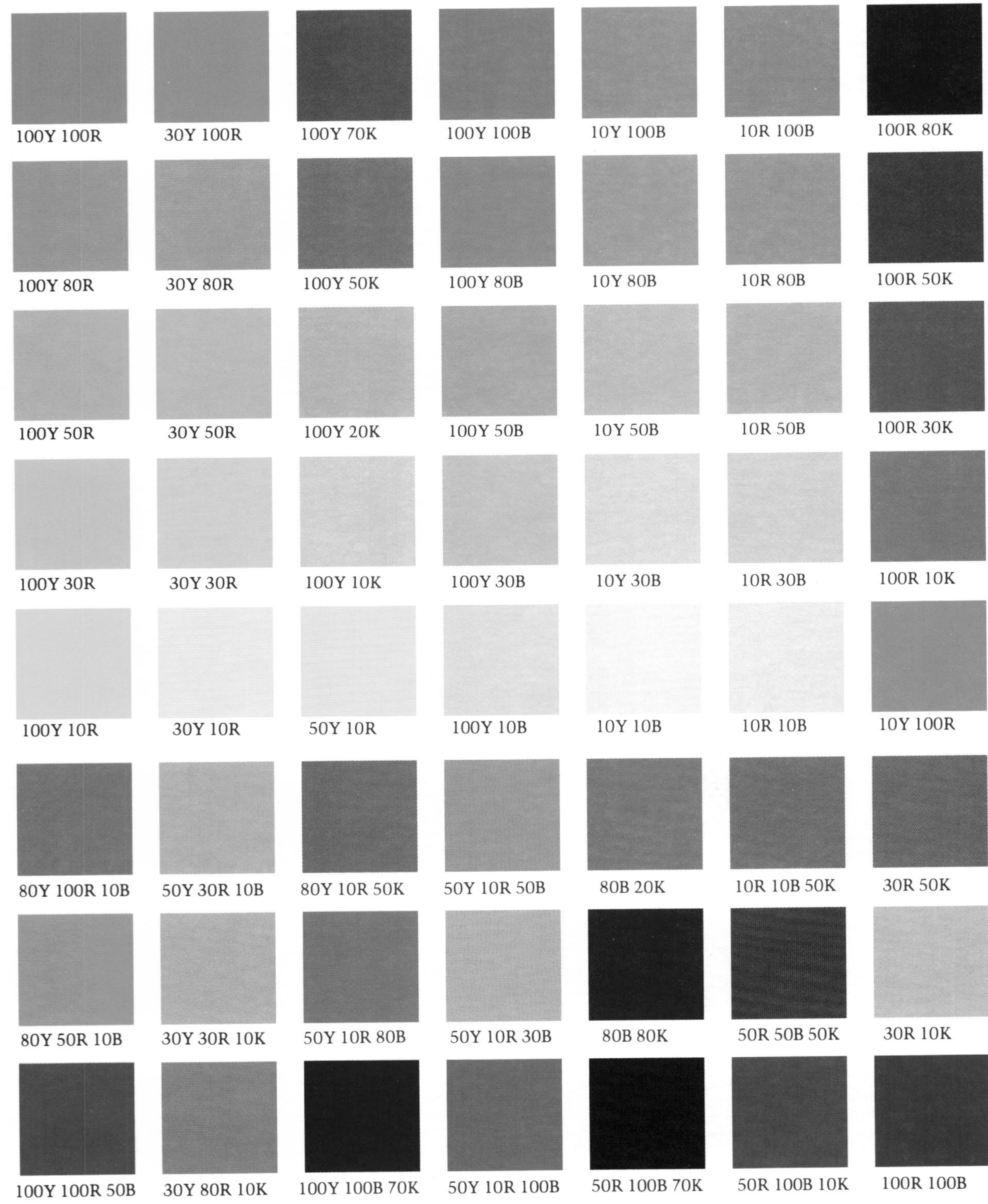

each color. To obtain these colors, the printer buys ink of the desired colors from an ink supplier; if special colors are required, the artist provides swatches which are matched by mixing standard inks and then given to the printer.

It is in the printing that special problems—and extra costs—arise. Each color is printed separately, which means—except in the case of multicolor presses that run several colors at the same time on different cylinders of the same machine—running the presses two, three, or four times, depending on the number of colors used. Between each press run, too, the presses must be thoroughly cleaned so that no trace is left of the last color used. This procedure is called washup.

A most serious problem, as it was for the illustrator in preseparation, is that of register. Great precision is obviously essential when any overprinting is involved, since the colors must combine exactly where indicated. Register can be faulty

Preseparated art by Giulio Maestro

A full-color sheet-fed press

due to improper mounting of the plates, irregular trimming of the paper, or, above all, distortion of the paper due to moisture. This can be caused by even a slight variation of humidity in the pressroom between the printing of each color, or by application of too much water in the course of the printing.

Proper register and color can only be checked by pulling proofs on the paper that will be used for printing, and then correcting the inking, the plates themselves, or the register. This, too, is an expensive operation, requiring great care and skill.

There are methods of flat-color printing that are less costly. One is the use of the above-mentioned multicolor presses, which, because each cylinder will be using the same color, do not require washup. They also save time in that one machine, though a more complicated one, can print all the necessary colors at once. Multicolor presses are widely used now, although at one time they were economical only for rather long print runs.

In register

Out of register

A FULL-COLOR WEB PRESS

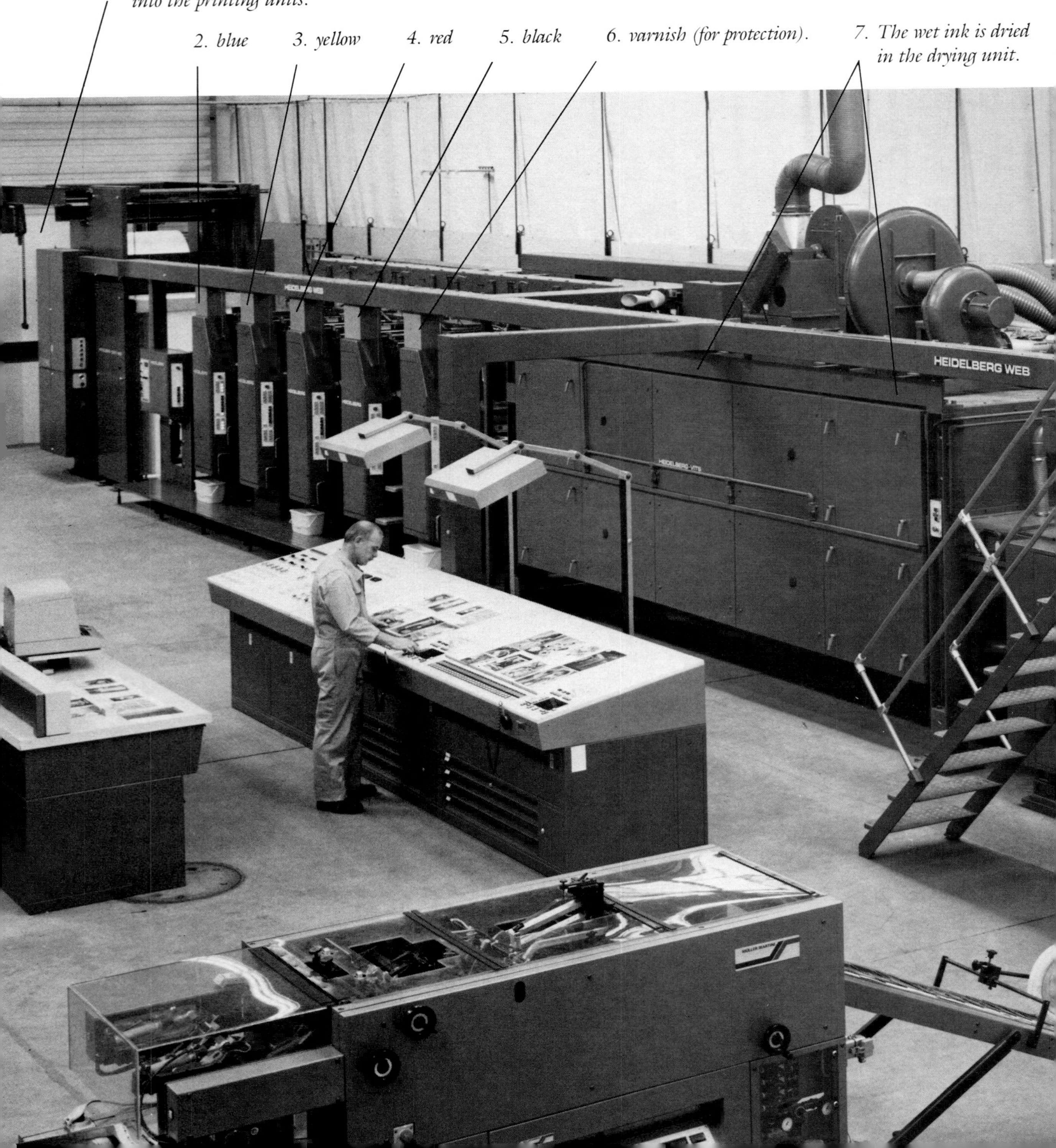

8. The web is slit the long way and then cut and folded into signatures.

9. The signatures move on a conveyer belt and are stacked up.

THE BINDER

Binding is the final step in the production of a book. Its purpose is to bring and hold together the printed pages of the book in the proper sequence, in some sort of permanent form, so that they will be protected within a case and can be read comfortably. The binder's job involves a mechanically complex operation, but it is relatively simple to understand, since each step leads logically to the final purpose. There are many such steps, and it is best to describe them one by one, although there are many machines used along the way that can carry out two or even more steps in one operation.

There are three common methods of bookbinding: edition binding, perfect binding, and notch or burst binding. They differ largely in that the pages are held together by sewing in the former and by an adhesive in the latter two.

The first step for all methods is the folding of the printed sheets, according to the predetermined imposition, or arrangement of the pages in the correct sequence for printing and binding. Once the sheets have been folded, they are called signatures. They generally contain sixteen or thirty-two pages. These individual signatures are then gathered, that is, they are assembled in the proper sequence for the book.

The next step is peculiar to edition binding. Edition-bound books are sewn, most often by a method called Smyth sewing. A thread of cotton, or sometimes nylon, is passed through the fold of each signature. It is then secured and passed through the stitches of other signatures so that all are joined together. This way of joining the signatures enables the book to be opened flat. Another method, known as side sewing, does not allow that. In this method, used generally for short books, often of no more than one or two signatures, the thread is passed through the entire book from the side. An advantage of side sewing is that it is less expensive than Smyth sewing; it is also very strong, but its very strength prevents the book from being opened flat.

In perfect binding, there is no sewing at all. Once used only for paperbacks and inexpensive books, it has in recent years been greatly improved, although it is still doubtful that perfect binding can ever be as durable as edition binding.

The backs of the signatures—the folding edges—are trimmed off, and the entire book becomes individual leaves. These edges are then made coarse, in order to increase the surface for the gluing which follows. Not only are one or two coats of a flexible adhesive applied to the edges, but a coarsely woven fabric is often attached to serve as added reinforcement.

Burst or notch binding is very much like perfect binding except that slits or cuts are made in the folded edges, which are not trimmed off. Glue is then forced into the slits, and the result is a binding that is said to be as strong as or stronger than edition binding.

The next step in the binding process, called smashing, is necessary only for edition binding. Since the back of the book has become slightly thicker because of the sewing thread, the volume must be brought to uniform thickness. This is accomplished by means of vertical presses that apply enormous pressure to the gathered signatures, squeezing out the air and compressing the pages firmly.

Gluing, which has already been done for perfect and notch or burst binding, follows smashing. In this process, a thin coat of flexible glue is applied to hold the signatures in place.

Next, the signatures are trimmed: that is, they are cut to their final size by means of trimming machines. The top, front, and bottom folds—all but the back ones—are opened up so that it will be possible to turn the pages.

At this point, it is possible to color the top edge of the book if desired. This procedure, called staining, though seldom done today, is worth mentioning. Putting a top stain on a book can be attractive esthetically; it also makes the book

PERFECT BINDING

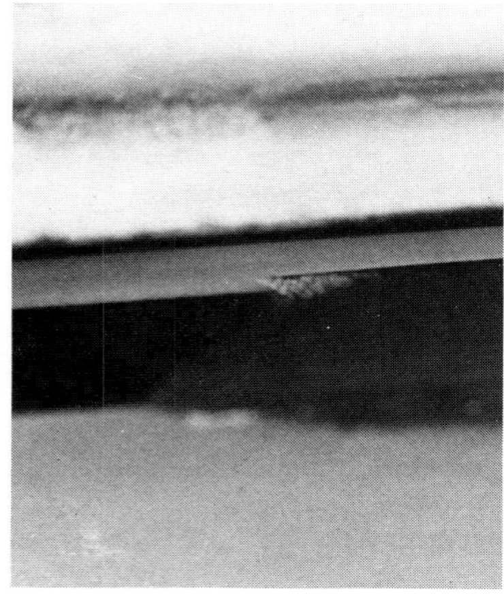

Back of signatures being trimmed off

Gluing

Cover being attached

look cleaner, and serves to make the edges of the paper dust resistant. Staining is done by brushing, sponging, or spraying the edges of the signatures with a water-soluble dye of any color.

The next two steps are commonly done on the same machine and concern preparation of the spine of the book; their aim is to enable the fastened-together signatures to be secured tightly within the covers.

The first of these two steps is called rounding. The backbone of the signatures is passed through a pair of rollers, which slightly rounds it, ensuring that the front edge of the book will remain under the covers and not protrude. This procedure, too, allows the covers to open and close easily.

The second of these steps is called backing, another way of making sure that the book will not slip out of its covers. By slightly widening and spreading out the back edge, backing provides joints for the book. In a way, it creates a sort of shoulder against which the covers of the book can fit.

The final step before actually putting the book in its cover now takes place. It is called lining up, and is often combined with the two previous operations. In lining up, one or more strips of gauze, known as crash or super, are glued to the back edge of the book. This cloth extends outward from both sides of the backbone. Very often, too, a strip of strong paper is also applied along the backbone. In this way the back of the book is reinforced and provided with a firm connection which will enable it to be attached to the covers.

Many years ago, headbands were attached to the backbone, extending slightly above the book, to protect the edges of fine binding materials such as leather. Today, headbands, though used, serve only a decorative purpose and are nothing more than very small pieces of cloth, woven with colored

EDITION BINDING

1. Press sheets are folded into signatures

2. Signatures are gathered

3. Signatures are Smyth sewn

4. Sewn signatures are reinforced with glue

5. Sewn signatures are trimmed

6. Sewn signatures are rounded (left) *and backed with paper* (right); *headbands are attached here*

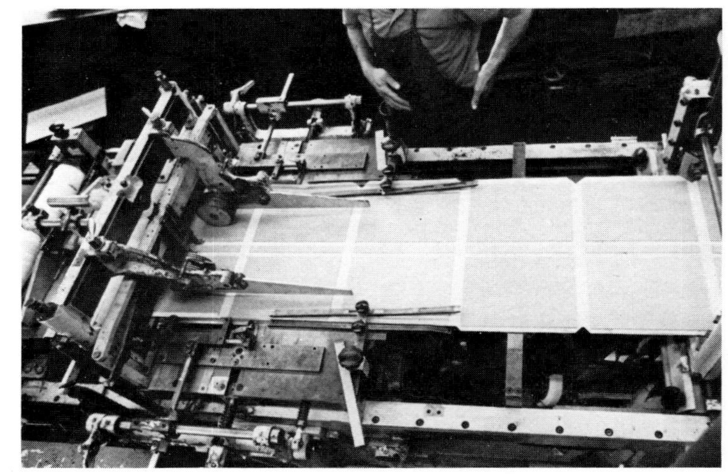

7. Cases are made and stamped

8. Signatures are cased-in

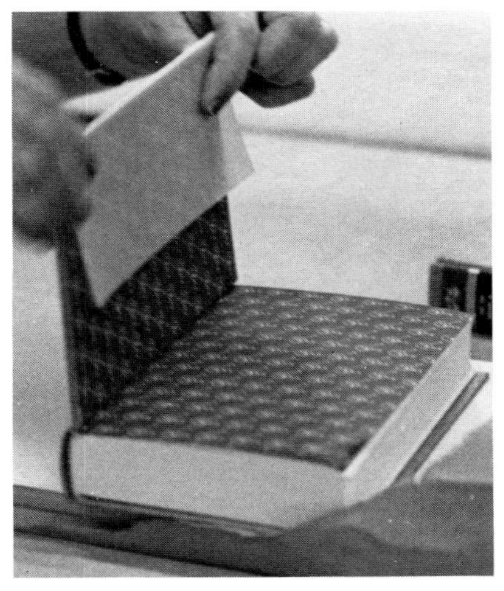

9. Books are jacketed, ready for shipping

thread, which are pasted to the lining material and protrude slightly to give a look of elegance to the book.

Whether sewn or glued together, the pages are now ready to be put between covers; the covers themselves are prepared while the sheets are folded, gathered, lined up, and so on, so that both are ready at the same time.

These covers—also called the case—serve several functions. They protect the book, allow it to stand on a shelf in a rigid position, make it durable, enhance its beauty, and provide other areas for information and identification.

Each cover consists of four parts: there are two boards, paper to line the backbone or spine, which is called backlining, and the cover material itself.

The boards are cut to a size slightly greater than that of the trim size of the book so that there will be a small, protective overlap. They are of a heavy cardboard, the strongest kind of which is called binder's board.

A heavy paper serves for the backlining. It is cut to a height slightly greater than that of the trim size and slightly wider than the bulk of the pages.

The cover material may be of cloth, plastic, or paper or a combination of cloth and paper. Cloth is the most durable covering. It is also the most expensive. Often a publisher will choose to use cloth for the center of the cover—the part that covers the spine and overlaps around the sides, which are subject to most wear—and paper for the rest of the cover in order to save money. The choice of the cover material—it is available in many grades, colors, and finishes—is made by the designer of the book, with both esthetic and economic considerations taken into account.

This cover material is cut to somewhat larger size than the boards to allow for folding over the edges (turn-in) and for extra material necessary for the joints.

Binding die

Once they have been chosen and cut, the parts of the cover are assembled. The inside of the cover material is coated with an adhesive; the boards and backlining are placed in proper position; and the extra material is folded over the edges by small rollers. All is then pressed firmly together.

Except for the addition of decorative or informative elements, the cover is finished. The information required is supplied by the editorial department, while its manner of presentation and any decorative aspects are decided upon by the designer.

Information to be placed on the spine generally includes the name of the author, the title of the book, and the name of the publisher. The back of the cover is usually blank, while the front cover might include a decoration or a symbol—occasionally the author's initials—for the book. Since it is a function of the jacket to convey the feeling of the book, covers tend to be simple. There are however, some exceptions, such as the occasional use of letterpress or offset to print elaborate illustrations on the cover material.

For the most part, printed matter and decorations are applied to the covers by means of stamping. There are two kinds of stamping, hot stamping and cold stamping; both make use of an etched plate called a binding die. Hot stamping is achieved by pressing the die against foil, or a leaf which is available in a large number of different colors. The metal die is heated, and the image is transferred to the cover material by means of heat. Hot stamping also includes blind stamping, which is the same process but without the use of foil. The impression is achieved by a difference in elevation, or relief images.

Cold stamping employs ink rather than foil. A deeply etched plate—the binding die—is inked, and the image is

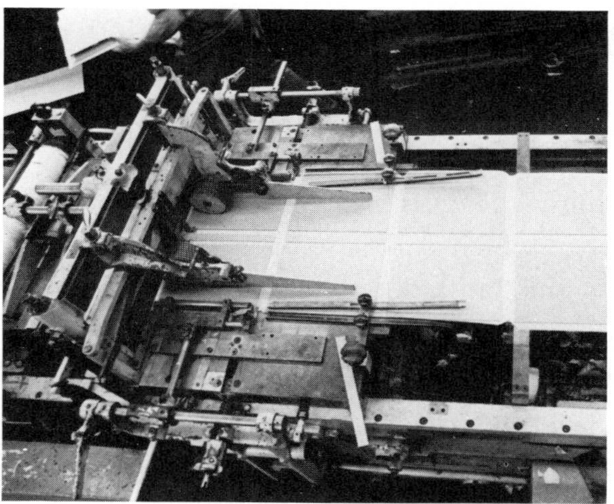

1. *Boards are glued in position on cloth*

2. *Cloth is cut and turned in*

3. *Cases are stamped*

4. *Three-piece case* (left) *and one-piece case* (right), *ready for casing-in*

transferred by great pressure sufficient to penetrate the cloth or paper cover material. This process is the same as ordinary letterpress, except that the pressure applied is far greater.

The book and its cover are now ready to be joined; this procedure is called casing in. The flat back of the case is slightly rounded by a heated bar, which corresponds in shape to the rounded backbone of the book. The outer leaves of the endpapers are covered with a glue or paste. The case is then placed around the book so that the boards are on the two endpapers, and two thin uncovered strips of the covering material are positioned over the joints of the book. The cased-in book is now firmly pressed to prevent warping of the boards. The press is hydraulic, and pressure is applied until the adhesive on the endpapers dries completely.

The result is a finished book. As it comes off the production line, each book is examined for faults and then jacketed, either by machine or by hand. It has been a long time between the author's conception of the work and the finished product.

Now the book must be shipped to the publisher's warehouse and sold. It must be promoted and publicized. Above all, it must be read.

FROM THE WAREHOUSE TO THE BOOKSTORE

Once the book has been printed, bound, and jacketed, there remains the final and all-important job of doing everything to see that it is sold to and read by as many people as possible. The first step is to move the books from the warehouse to the stores; the second will be to move them from the stores into the homes of the customers. These two goals are worked on simultaneously in many ways, but they can be most clearly discussed separately.

Seeing that the book reaches the stores is primarily the task of the sales representatives. The sales reps first learn about the book at a meeting called a sales conference, usually held before the book is finished. Most publishers divide their lists into two seasons but others divide them into three or more seasons.

Present at these meetings are many members of the publishing house: members of the editorial staff, the publicity department, representatives of the advertising agency, and of course the entire sales force. During the sales conference, which, depending on the size of the list, can last one, two, or even three days, future books are discussed and presented to the reps so that they may have all the information necessary to sell the books.

Each title—and it is essential to remember that each title is a distinct product, different from all others—is presented to the reps by an editor, the publisher, or, in some cases, the sales manager who directs and coordinates the activities of the entire sales force. Presentations are generally made in the order in which each book appears in the catalog of future titles which has been prepared in the publishing house before the sales conference and which will be an important sales tool.

The reps will want to know just what the book is about and, essentially, why a bookstore, and in the end a customer, should buy it. In other words, they want a "handle" for each book. This means quite simply a short (the shorter the better) description of those qualities that should make a book salable. For example, it is the first biography of some prominent and interesting figure; it is a book that has been sold to the movies; it is a work of literature of such importance that it is certain to be widely reviewed and praised; and so on.

Information about the author is useful, and a book's special appeal to a specific area of the country—whether it be the author's birthplace, residence, or the setting of the book—will be discussed. The reps will want to know what the publicity department plans to do for the book, whether or not excerpts from it have been sold to a magazine for publication before the book is published, whether or not it is a book club selection, and what the advertising budget will be. Essential to the reps, too, is knowledge of the size of the first printing. This could be discussed and even revised at the sales conference, depending upon the reactions of those attending the meeting to any given title, but usually the number of copies to be printed has been determined in advance. This figure is an important one to the reps since it reflects the publisher's confidence in the book.

Of great importance is the presentation of each jacket to the members of the sales conference. Usually, it is a color proof of the jacket that is prepared and shown so that suggestions made by the sales staff and others can be followed before the jacket is printed. Occasionally, the reps will be presented with a number of different comps for a title, and the selection of the final jacket will be discussed by all those attending the conference. A most effective jacket might be the result of such an exchange of ideas.

The sales conference is basically a period set aside for an exchange of ideas, of ways in which a title can best be sold to the stores. By the end of these meetings, the reps should be fully prepared to present each book, to tell each bookstore owner or buyer why each title should be bought, and to answer any question that might be asked. Above all, the presentation of a book at the sales conference should generate interest. The jacket might be good, the "handle" useful, but the enthusiasm that one person—usually the editor—can convey to the sales force can well mean the difference in the end between a book that sells well and one that sells poorly.

Once the sales meetings are over, the reps gather together their materials in preparation for the selling trip. These materials consist of a jacket (or proof of one) for each book, a catalog of all the new titles as well as of the backlist (those books published in the past that might be reordered), and a number of order forms. In the case of heavily illustrated books, it could be useful to carry along a sample illustration or two; for

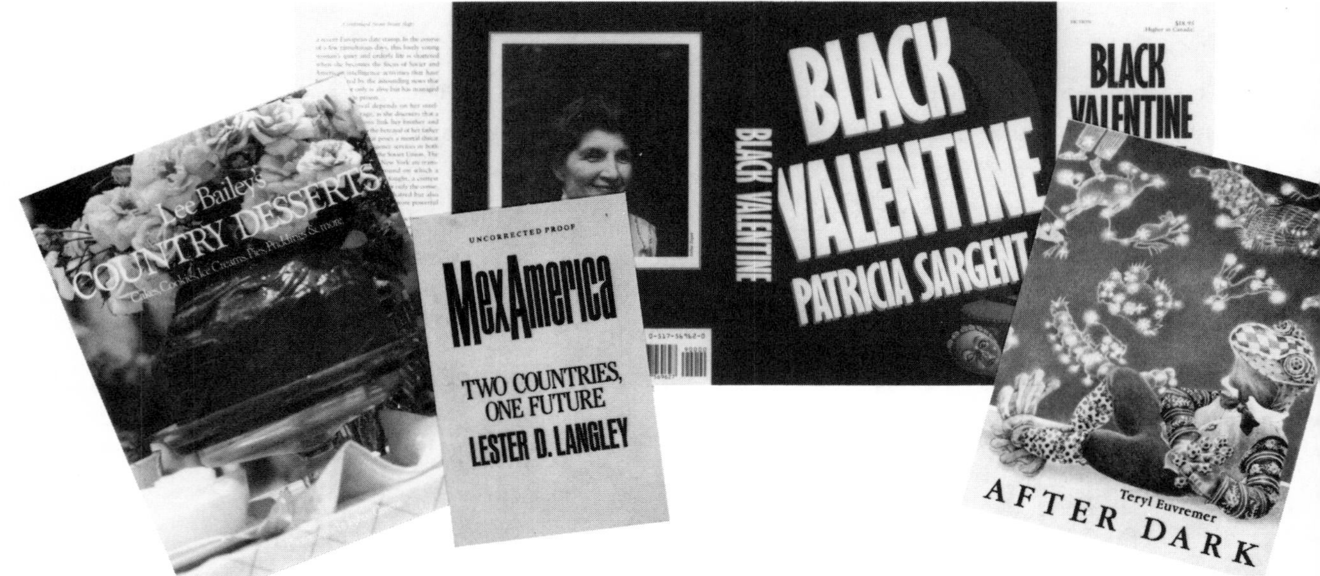

Jackets, bound galleys, and sample signatures are used by sales reps to sell books before they are completed

children's books, an unbound copy of the book itself is helpful since the appearance of the entire book is of great importance to a bookseller.

Most reps are "house" reps; that is, they sell for only one publisher who pays a salary, expenses, and occasionally a commission on sales. There are, however, commission reps who sell for a number of different publishers—the smaller publishers which cannot afford to keep a full-time sales force. These reps pay their own expenses and receive as compensation a percentage of the sales. This commission is generally between 10 and 12½ percent of the wholesale price on sales to bookstores (generally 60 percent of the retail price charged to the customer) and between 5 and 7½ percent of the price to wholesalers.

All of these reps sell to three basic types of accounts. First of all, there are the bookstores—small personal ones, as well as large chains which usually buy their books through one central office. Then there are the wholesalers who buy in large quantities and in turn sell these books to retail stores and libraries. Many small shops prefer to buy from wholesalers since the latter carry books of all publishers, and thus billing and accounting procedures are simplified. The wholesalers, too, are generally located in or close to large cities where they have their warehouses, so they can usually supply books more quickly than can individual publishers. The third type of account is the library. Libraries most often buy from wholesalers, but certain library systems prefer to purchase their books directly from the publisher. Libraries constitute 85 percent of the market for children's books and approximately 10 percent of adult books.

By the time they are ready to begin their selling trips, the reps should be thoroughly familiar with each title they will present to the booksellers. The shorter, more concise, and more informative the presentation, the better the rep is able to sell the right number of copies to each store. Because of the large number of books carried by each rep, there is a strictly limited amount of time that can be devoted to any single title. Within this limited amount of time, the bookstore buyers will want to know, just as the reps wanted to know from the publishers, just how each title can best be sold to their customers. The annual American Booksellers Association convention is attended by a large number of booksellers, publishers, and reps. Here booksellers are able to learn not only what books are coming from all publishers, but which of that number will be highlighted, and how each publisher will aid and support—through promotion, publicity, and advertising—those titles. However, the personal touch of the individual rep plays an important part in the decisions of each bookstore buyer. The rep must know the individual needs of each

Catalogs

INDIAN GIVERS

HOW THE INDIANS OF THE AMERICAS TRANSFORMED THE WORLD

By Jack Weatherford

OCTOBER

Not until we discover intelligent life elsewhere in the universe will there be an event comparable in importance to the collision of the Indian New World with the European Old World. The staggering variety of plants discovered there means that three-fifths of what humans eat today came from the Americas, not to mention the drugs that get us high, the democratic institutions we regard as "European," the kind of sex we have—in fact, the very wealth that made the industrial revolution possible and shaped key modern institutions.

Weatherford shows, by visiting contemporary sites of Indian societies past and present, that we are still learning from the Native Americans, about everything from agriculture to medicine, from religion to fashion. We may have forgotten or misunderstood far more about these "Indian givers" than we know today. How we live and how we earn a living were all influenced by the interrelating process that began the minute Europeans stepped out of their galleons to discover the Americas.

Mixing contemporary observations and history, brilliant anecdotes and painstaking scholarship, anthropologist Jack Weatherford has written a fascinating account of the price the Indians paid to transform world civilization. *Indian Givers* is an ideal gift for readers wondering why we live the way we do.

Jack Weatherford, author of *Tribes on the Hill* and *Porn Row*, is professor of anthropology at Macalester College in St. Paul, Minnesota.

Anthropology/History
6 x 9/288 pages
Crown
569698. $17.95 hardcover
Canada: $24.95 hardcover

INDIAN
GIVERS
HOW
THE INDIANS
OF THE
AMERICAS
TRANSFORMED
THE WORLD
JACK WEATHERFORD

WHALE NATION

By Heathcote Williams

Heathcote Williams's Whale Nation is an astonishing evocation in verse and pictures of whales and dolphins, the ocean, the earth, and the universe. Hailed by playwright Harold Pinter ("It's wonderful"), the book is by turns dazzlingly beautiful and shockingly brutal.

The poem portrays the entire being of the Leviathan—its ancient origins, its songs and play, its mating rituals, and its relationship to its young—reminding us that "the planet is the territory, not of humans, but of the whale." It includes a remarkable collection of prose from the worlds of science and literature—from Aristotle to Carl Sagan—showing how these animals have inspired the greatest thinkers in history.

"Large creatures disappear, life becomes smaller," writes Williams as he illustrates the many ways the whales have contributed to modern life, from providing fuel for the industrial revolution to controlling the oceans' plankton population helping to maintain the earth's atmosphere.

Whale Nation invites all readers to share this celebration of the whale and be touched by an overwhelming call for compassion for these creatures and for the "civilization built on the back of the whale."

Heathcote Williams has gained an international reputation as an award-winning playwright and as an accomplished screenplay writer and actor. He lives in England.

Nature/Conservation
150 full-color and black-and-white photographs
7¾ x 11¾/208 pages
A Harmony Book
569329. $25.00 hardcover
NCR

bookstore—each shop has its own character—and the store's buyer must have confidence in the reliability and integrity of each rep.

The larger the order that a shop or wholesaler gives, the greater the discount. A usual discount to a bookstore would be 20 percent for an order of a single copy of a book, and over 42 percent for a very substantial order. The discount to a wholesaler is, of course, higher, averaging 46 percent, since the wholesaler itself will be selling books to retailers at a discount.

Nonetheless, it is not to the publisher's advantage to ship an unrealistically high number of copies of a book, and because of this a wise rep will make no effort to oversell any one title. The reason for this is that all books sold to a bookstore (and to wholesalers) are returnable: that is, the copies not sold by a store can be returned to the publisher for credit. The rep may place a very large number of copies of any one title in the stores only to find that they remain unsold to customers and are eventually returned to the publisher. Obviously, unless the rep keeps in touch with the stores to find out if the books are moving out of the stores and into the hands of customers, and conveys this information to the publisher, the latter could bring out a second printing of a title when the first was far from sold out.

Overbuying, in spite of return privileges, is unprofitable for the bookseller as well, since there are certain conditions attached to the return of books to the publisher. A soiled or damaged book cannot be returned for credit; there is a time limit for returns; and return shipping costs must be paid for by the bookseller. In addition, the amount of paperwork involved can be more time-consuming than it is worth. As careful as reps and booksellers are, approximately 25 percent of

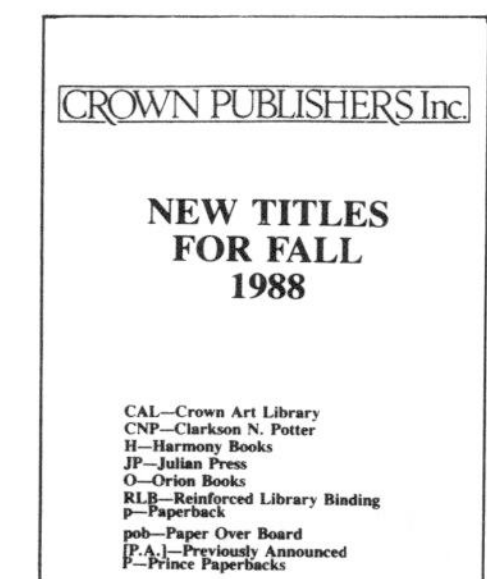

CROWN PUBLISHERS Inc.

NEW TITLES FOR FALL 1988

CAL—Crown Art Library
CNP—Clarkson N. Potter
H—Harmony Books
JP—Julian Press
O—Orion Books
RLB—Reinforced Library Binding
p—Paperback
pob—Paper Over Board
[P.A.]—Previously Announced
P—Prince Paperbacks

HC7 | ACCOUNT NUMBER | CUSTOMER REF NO | TOTAL UNITS | COM | DISCOUNT UNITS | GENERAL DISCOUNT | ADV DISC | B O INSTR | SLSMN NO
A O D | SHIPPING DATE | SPEC SALE | DEPT NO | R | SHIPPING CHARGE | DATE SHIPPED | VIA CD | VIA NAME | CREDIT DEPT

CROWN PUBLISHERS, INC. 225 PARK AVENUE SOUTH, NEW YORK, N.Y. 10003 $50.00 MINIMUM Toll Free Ordering—1-800-526-4264 In N J Call—201-382-7600 ext 119 SALES & TITLE INFORMATION—201-382-7600 ext 119 DATE

YOUR ACCOUNT NUMBER | SHIP TO
BILL TO
ADDRESS
CITY & STATE
MARK FOR ZIP | MARK FOR ZIP
ORDER NO | DEPT NO | DISCOUNT | WHEN SHIP | SHIP VIA | SPECIAL INSTRUCTIONS

TERMS 2/10 EOM NET 30 F O B SHIPPING POINT
MINIMUM TRADE ORDER $30.00 NET PRICES SUBJECT TO CHANGE WITHOUT NOTICE
☐ PAYMENT ENCLOSED $______
☐ CHARGE MY ESTABLISHED ACCOUNT
☐ NEW ACCOUNTS PLEASE SUBMIT TRADE AND BANKING REFERENCE PRE PAYMENT OF YOUR FIRST ORDER WILL INSURE PROMPT DELIVERY
ALL AUTHORIZED RETURNS ARE FOR CREDIT ONLY AND MAY BE APPLIED AGAINST FUTURE PURCHASES

BACK ORDER INSTRUCTIONS
☐ USUAL BILL AND SHIP AS READY
☐ CANCEL PREVIOUS BACK ORDER FOR TITLES ON THIS ORDER
☐ CANCEL ALL UNAVAILABLE BOOKS EXCEPT NEW PUBS AS OF ______
☐ CANCEL ALL UNAVAILABLE BOOKS INCL NEW PUBS AS OF ______
ISBN PREFIX 0-517

BUYER | INVOICE NO
BUYERS PHONE
SALES REP AND NUMBER

Item No. Quan. — Title — Price

August

Judith Krantz

570262 ____ Till We Meet Again, *Krantz* 19.95
Available in 12-copy cartons.
570769 ____ **FLOOR DISPLAY, 18-copy:** Till We Meet Again, *Krantz* 359.10

570068 ____ Lanterns Across the Snow, *Hill* ......(CNP) 13.95
571080 **PREPACK, 6-copy:** Lanterns Across the Snow, *Hill* ....(CNP) 83.70
569620 ____ Black Valentine, *Sargeant* 18.95
569191 ____ Thoughts While Tending Sheep, *Ilefeldt* 15.95
568071 ____ Safe Passage, *Bache* 16.95
569701 ____ Ringer, *Thayer* 18.95
567822 ____ House of Heroes and Other Stories, *La Chapelle* 16.95

The Crown Art Library
August

537400 ____ Cassatt, *Roudebush* ....(CAL) 12.95
503026 ____ Klee, *Chevalier* ....(CAL) 12.95
00500X ____ Van Gogh, *Huyghe* ....(CAL) 12.95

November

004992 ____ Gauguin, *Huyghe* ....(CAL) 12.95
558726 ____ Hundertwasser, *Mathey* ....(CAL) 12.95
03722X ____ Manet, *Rey* ....(CAL) 12.95
516713 ____ Miró, *Diehl* ....(CAL) 12.95
515717 ____ Munch, *Selz* ....(CAL) 12.95
See Backlist Order Form for the complete Crown Art Library list.

568446 ____ Combat Aircraft of World War II, Vol. V: 1941–1942, *Angelucci and Matricardi* (O) 17.95
568454 ____ Combat Aircraft of World War II, Vol. VI: 1942–1943, *Angelucci and Matricardi* (O) 17.95
568462 ____ Combat Aircraft of World War II, Vol. VII: 1943–1944, *Angelucci and Matricardi* (O) 17.95
568470 ____ Combat Aircraft of World War II, Vol. VIII: 1944–1945, *Angelucci and Matricardi* (O) 17.95
56792X ____ Jaguar, *Porter* ....(O) 40.00
568640 ____ Tiger Moth, *McKay* ....(O) 18.95
569361 ____ Homespun, *Smith* **[P.A.—Avail. October]** .. 19.95

September

568993 ____ Legacy of Lace, *Warnick and Nilsson* 24.95
570483 ____ How to Buy Great Shoes That Fit, *Norman* ....(P) p 5.95
570491 ____ **PREPACK, 10-copy:** How to Buy Great Shoes That Fit, *Norman* ....(P) p 59.50
564386 ____ Brontës, The, *Fraser* 25.00
570297 ____ In an Irish House, *Connolly* ....(H) 40.00
570386 ____ Martin Leman's Comic and Curious Cats, *Leman* ....(H) p 6.95
568632 ____ Off-Hollywood Movies, *Skorman* .....(H) p 10.95
569507 ____ Away for the Weekend™: New England, Revised Edition, *Berman* ....(CNP) p 11.95
569841 ____ Third Century, The, *Kotkin and Kishimoto* .. 19.95

Ralph and Terry Kovel

56985X ____ Kovel's Antiques & Collectibles Price List, 21st Edition, *Kovel* ....p 10.95
See Backlist Order Form for the complete Kovel book list.

569183 ____ Men at Sea, *Aymar* 24.95
569418 ____ Labor Pains, *Klimo* 16.95
569892 ____ Mary Emmerling's American Country Hearts, *Emmerling* ......(CNP) slipcased 12.95
570629 ____ **PREPACK, 10-copy:** Mary Emmerling's American Country Hearts, *Emmerling* ....(CNP) slipcased 129.50

Barbara Milo Ohrbach

570211 ____ Memories of Childhood, *Ohrbach* ....(CNP) 8.95
570475 ____ **COUNTER DISPLAY, 12-copy:** Memories of Childhood, *Ohrbach* ....(CNP) 107.40

Also Available

56081X ____ Scented Room, The *Ohrbach* ....(CNP) 17.95
566575 ____ Token of Friendship, A., *Ohrbach* ...(CNP) 8.95

October

570661 ____ Beatles, The: Recording Sessions, *Lewisohn* ....(H) 24.95
569299 ____ This Is Your Life, *Wolitzer* 17.95

The Crown Insider's Guides™

569000 ____ Crown Insiders' Guide™ to Italy: 1988–1989, *Hults* ....p 10.95
568608 ____ Crown Insiders' Guide™ to the Caribbean: 1988–1989, *Puzzo, Lemkowitz, and Raskin* ....p 10.95
See Backlist Order Form for the complete Crown Insiders' Guides™ list.

570963 ____ Complete Illustrated Book of Yoga, The, *Vishnudevananda* ....(H) p 10.95
570955 ____ Complete Illustrated Book of Yoga, The, *Vishnudevananda* ....(H) 20.00
569752 ____ Latin Riddle Book, The, *Phillips* ....(H) 9.95
569736 ____ Laura Ashley at Home, *Ashley, Jackson, Haig, Irvine, Clifford, and Greene* ...(H) 30.00
569636 ____ Screen World: 1988, Volume 39, *Willis* 29.95
570548 ____ Total Garden, The, *Clevely* ....(H) 25.00
570289 ____ President's Women, The, *Singer* 18.95

The Cat Books
Muncaster and Sawyer

568918 ____ *Black* Cat Made Me Buy It!, The, *Muncaster and Sawyer* ....p 12.95

Also Available

553384 ____ Cat Made Me Buy It!, The, *Muncaster and Sawyer* ....p 8.95
563037 ____ Cat Sold It!, The, *Muncaster and Sawyer* ..p 9.95

569809 ____ Architect in Italy, An, *Mauduit* ......(CNP) 14.95

Sheila Pickles

57098X ____ Love, *Pickles* ....(H) slipcased 18.95

Also Available

567660 ____ Victorian Posy, A, *Pickles* .....(H) slipcased 17.95

56954X ____ Soviet Manned Space Program, The, *Clark* ....(O) 24.95
567482 ____ Doolittle Raid, The, *Glines* ....(O) 17.95
569205 ____ U.S. Navy Aircraft 1921–1941 and U.S. Marine Corps Aircraft 1914-1959, *Larkins* ....(O) 27.50
566753 ____ Battle of Hurtgen Forest, The, *Whiting* ..(O) 18.95
569698 ____ Indian Givers, *Weatherford* 17.95
569329 ____ Whale Nation, *Williams* ....(H) 25.00
569523 ____ Guadalcanal: Decision at Sea, *Hammel* 24.95
57084X ____ Signal, *Kelly* ....(H) p 16.95
569167 ____ Tuscan in the Kitchen, A, *Luongo with Hederman and Raives* ....(CNP) 22.95
560178 ____ Italian Country, *Sabino* ....(CNP) 35.00
569744 ____ Private Gardens of Scotland, *Truscott* ....(H) 50.00
568748 ____ Greek Style, *Slesin, Cliff, and Rozensztroch* ....(CNP) 35.00
568233 ____ Etiquette: Charlotte Ford's Book of Modern Manners, *Ford* **[P.A.]** ....(CNP) 25.00
570300 ____ Columbia University College of Physicians and Surgeons Complete Guide to Pregnancy, The, *Staff of College of Physicians and Surgeons* 24.95
568985 ____ Peter Gowland's *New* Handbook of Glamour Photography, *Gowland with Gowland* ... 19.95
570785 ____ Disney Studio Story, The, *Holliss and Sibley* 35.00
570351 ____ Super Skin, *Novick* ....(CNP) 18.95
570327 ____ Larousse Gastronomique, *Lang* 50.00

November

560011 ____ Man Ray, *Baldwin* ....(CNP) 25.00

CROWN VIDEO
Martha Stewarts Secrets for Entertaining

570904 ____ Holiday Feast for Thanksgiving and Other Festive Occasions, A, *Stewart* ..... VHS 24.95
569825 ____ Antipasto Party, An, *Stewart* .... VHS 24.95

Also Available

569124 ____ Buffet Party for Family and Friends, A, *Stewart* ....VHS 24.95
569140 ____ Formal Dinner Party, A, *Stewart* ......VHS 24.95

565668 ____ Wedding Planner, The, *Stewart*, ...(CNP) hidden spiral bound, slipcased 30.00
570270 ____ Vicars of Christ, *De Rosa* 18.95
57019X ____ Vietnam Veterans Memorial, The, *Katakis* .. 15.95
568780 ____ New York Son, *Feder* 16.95
568942 ____ Quilting Together, *Nadelstern and Hancock* . 35.00
560798 ____ Pierre Deux's Normandy, *Dannenberg, Le Vec, and Moulin* ....(CNP) 35.00
570572 ____ Walt Disney and Assorted Other Characters, *Kinney* ....(H) 16.95
570637 ____ Bears, *Picot and Picot* ....(H) 35.00
570556 ____ Best of Crime & Detective TV, *Collins and Javna* ....(H) p 8.95
570084 ____ Selling Your Screenplay, *Whitcomb* 15.95
57005X ____ Special Occasions *Hadamuscin* ....(H) 22.50
570777 ____ Into the Woods, *Sondheim, Lapine and Talbott* 24.95
566176 ____ Sub vs. Sub, *Compton-Hall* ....(O) 24.95

CHILDREN'S BOOKS

Raffi

568063 ____ Raffi Christmas Treasury, The *Raffi* (September) ....RLB 17.95
See the Backlist Order Form for the complete Raffi list.

566311 ____ Twelve Gifts for Santa Claus, *Kunnas* (September) ....RLB 10.95
565986 ____ Little Tree, *cummings* (September) .....RLB 9.95
570823 ____ **PREPACK, 10-copy:** Little Tree, *cummings* (September) ....RLB 99.50
558181 ____ Santa Claus and His Elves, *Kunnas* (September) ....p 4.95
559439 ____ **PREPACK, 12-copy:** Santa Claus and His Elves, *Kunnas* (September) ....p 49.50
569566 ____ Our Soccer League, *Solomon* (September) ....RLB 11.95
569817 ____ First Book of Football, The, *Madden* (September) ....pob 10.95
568292 ____ We Keep a Pig in the Parlor, *Bloom* (October) ....(CNP) 13.95
569965 ____ Alexander and the Dragon, *Holabird and Craig* (September) ....(CNP) 9.95
570602 ____ Hidden Life of the Pond, The, *Schwartz* (October) ....RLB 12.95
570580 ____ Hidden Life of the Forest, The, *Schwartz* (October) ....RLB 12.95
570599 ____ Hidden Life of the Meadow, The, *Schwartz* (October) ....RLB 12.95
569582 ____ Dollars and Cents for Harriet, *Maestro* (September) ....RLB 12.95
569973 ____ Rabbits on Roller Skates!, *Wahl* (August) ....RLB 6.95
570432 ____ Thomas the Tortoise, *Jeffrey* (September) ... 9.95
566974 ____ My Family Vacation, *Khalsa* (September) ....(CNP) RLB 12.95
569779 ____ Our Changing World: The Rock Pool, *Bellamy* (October) ....(CNP) 9.95
569760 ____ Our Changing World: The Roadside, *Bellamy* (October) ....(CNP) 9.95
570017 ____ Alexandra Ingredient, The, *Strauss* (October) 12.95
568411 ____ Books: From Writer to Reader, Revised and Updated Edition, *Greenfeld* (November) p 12.95
568403 ____ Books: From Writer to Reader, Revised and Updated Edition, *Greenfeld* (November) . 19.95

Parents Magazine Press (July)

570181 ____ Pickle Things, *Brown* ....p 2.95
570165 ____ Aren't You Forgetting Something, Fiona?, *Cole* ....p 2.95
570157 ____ Henry Goes West, *Quackenbush* ....p 2.95
570130 ____ Socks for Supper, *Kent* ....p 2.95
570173 ____ Buggly Bear's Hiccup Cure, *Kelley* ....p 2.95
570149 ____ Pets I Wouldn't Pick, *Schmeltz* ....p 2.95
883317 ____ **FLOOR DISPLAY, 60-copy:** Empty display. Order books individually. ...... Free
See Backlist Order Form for the complete Parents Magazine Press list.

Item No	Quan	Title

Item No	Quan	Title

Prices subject to change without notice. When using your own purchase order, please include item numbers with complete titles. TOLL FREE ORDERS: $50.00 net value; please supply stock numbers and have order prepared before placing phone call.

WHITE RETURN TO CROWN YELLOW RETURN TO CROWN PINK SALES REP COPY GOLD CUSTOMER'S COPY 5/488/

Book order form

CROWN PUBLISHERS Inc.

CROWN PUBLISHERS, INC. CLARKSON N. POTTER, INC. HARMONY BOOKS

TRADE DISCOUNT SCHEDULE

Forward all orders to:	Cash discount:	Address for returns:
Crown Publishers, Inc. 225 Park Ave., South New York, N.Y. 10003	2/10 EOM, net 30. All shipments FOB Warehouse, Avenel, N.J.	Crown Publishers, Inc. Returns Department 34 Engelhard Avenue Avenel, N.J. 07001

Cloth & Paper - Single and Assorted
New and Backlist Titles

1-4 copies	20%
5-9 copies	40%
10-24 copies	42%
25-49 copies	44%
50-99 copies	45%
100-999 copies	46%
1,000-1,499 copies	47%
1,500 and up copies	48%

Minimum Order: $50.00 net.

RETURN POLICY: Publisher permits return of overstock under the following conditions: Bookseller must supply a dated packing slip listing item numbers, titles, quantities and retail unit prices. No permission necessary. Returns accepted on mint condition only. NOP and non-returnable titles will be returned and charged back at bookseller's expense. A 10% handling charge will be added if the bookseller's price and season letter markings, ink, pencil and gum labels are not completely removed. Scheduled charges will be applied to entire shipment if any price markings are not removed. Collect returns will be refused.

Return damaged and defective books with invoice information and statement of defects. No return penalty.

Period of Eligibility: Not before 6 months nor later than 1 year from date of invoice.

Credit Allowed: All returns will be credited at 53% except first novels. First novels will be credited at purchased discount. All books must be in saleable condition and shipped post-paid to our warehouse address. No credit will be issued on receipt of shopworn books. All returns are for credit only and may be applied against future purchases.

POLICY CONCERNING REBATES: On original editions of reprint titles, rebates will be granted provided that the original edition has not been out of print 6 months or longer.

Living Language™, (P) Prince Paperback, (AH) Arlington House, (AW) American West, (B) Barre, (By) Bounty, (JP) Julian Press, (WR) Ward Ritchie, dilithium press.
688

225 PARK AVENUE SOUTH, NEW YORK, NEW YORK 10003 • 212 254-1600 • TELEX 427195

Trade discount schedule

all books sold to bookstores in the United States are eventually returned to the publishers.

Reps are an essential link between the publishing house and the bookseller. They are important not only as the persons who sell books, but also as those in the best position to carry information from publisher to bookseller and from bookseller to publisher, thus enabling both to perform their jobs more effectively.

FROM THE BOOKSTORE TO THE READER

Once the book has been sold to the stores—and usually well before that—the publicity department begins working (together with other members of the publishing house, when necessary) to do everything possible to see that the books move out of the stores and into the readers' homes. When the question is asked, "What makes a book sell?" the usual reply is "Word of mouth," and generating word of mouth is the job of the publicity department. The original product, the book itself, should be so interesting and informative that it will lead one reader to recommend it to another, but the initial interest in the book must be stimulated by the publishing house's publicity department.

Ideally, the publicity director should be intelligent, with an attractive personality (for that job is essentially one of public relations) and a deep interest in books. A publicity director should have contacts with newspaper, magazine, and television people, and should preferably be on good terms

Scribner's bookstore in New York City

with book reviewers. Above all, however, a publicity director must be creative and imaginative, because a new approach or a new idea to be used in publicizing the book could well mean the difference between its commercial success and failure. It is very often impossible to explain why one book sells and another doesn't, but publicity directors must draw on all their skills and imagination to call attention to the publication—and merits—of each book.

These efforts fall within the scope of spreading word of mouth, and the almost infinite ways of achieving this are impossible to discuss here, since each book is a unique product and requires, ideally, a unique approach. Nonetheless, there are a few basic steps essential to the publicizing of any book, and these, with a brief look at others, are worth describing.

The most important tool in publicizing a book is the book itself, because only the book itself can stimulate the necessary enthusiasm. It is important that the publicity director, or at least a member of the staff, read the book either in manuscript or in galleys. This is obviously not always possible—a large house publishes very many books—but it is desirable, and a book should at least be skimmed even if not carefully read. In this way, the publicity department is better able to generate interest in the book out of its own genuine enthusiasm.

There are basically two areas of book publicity. The first is through reviews and book news columns in newspapers and magazines; the second, popularly called "off the book page," is anything other than book reviews or book news. Procedures for this first method of publicizing a book are pretty much standard. A book might first be announced by means of a press release: a short statement is sent to magazines and newspapers—most importantly *Publishers Weekly,* the indus-

TRADE NEWS

EDITED BY WILLIAM GOLDSTEIN

HARDCOVER BOOKS

Continuum Signs Paul And Jeanne Simon for Books on Presidential Race

Continuum has signed former presidential candidate Senator Paul Simon and his wife Jeanne to separate contracts for two books concerning the 1988 presidential campaign. The Illinois senator will look at the 1988 election from the Iowa primary through the November election, in **Winners and Losers: The Race for the Presidency 1988**, to be published after the inauguration of the new president in late January 1989. Jeanne Simon's book is tentatively titled **Codename "Scarlett": The Campaign Diary of Jeanne Simon**, a reference to the name the Secret Service gave to Mr. Simon during the campaign. Mrs. Simon's book is based on a journal she kept during her husband's campaign; written in diary form, it also includes personal reflections on her experience written specifically for publication. *Codename "Scarlett"* is scheduled for April 1989.

Simon told *PW* that he is writing the book because "I feel that a book that not only tells the story of the campaign, but also reflects on the weaknesses and strengths of the process is in order." He sees the deficiencies of the system as "how we finance campaigns, and the focus of the media on the trivia and horse-race aspect rather than the issues.

"I think it's a problem that Americans are no longer issue-oriented and it's a problem that feeds on itself. If there's little interest, and the media doesn't provide information, there's even less interest. There's an important leadership role that the media has to take," he added.

In *Winners and Losers*, Senator Simon will review the various candidates' campaigns (including his own), explore how political strategies were made, reveal what the families endured, and such behind-the-scenes information as what the candidates said to each other after each debate. Simon will also cover the Democratic and Republican conventions and the election itself, analyzing the winner's character and discussing what his election will mean for the country. Simon expects to finish the bulk of his book by Labor Day, then add "a chapter or two" on the election itself. In his estimation, the winner will be Dukakis. "It'll be close but I think he has a real shot."

The senator was trained as a journalist; he left college at the age of 19 to edit a Southern Illinois newspaper. Before long, he owned a chain of 14 papers, but he wanted to do more in the way of public service. He then entered politics, eventually becoming a U.S. representative in 1975, U.S. senator in 1985, and a Democratic presidential candidate in 1988. He has written 10 books, including *Lincoln's Preparation for Greatness*, *The Tongue-Tied American*, a book on America's foreign-language crisis, and an inspirational book for young people, *Beginnings*. He also co-authored a book with his wife about Protestant-Catholic marriages. (Simon is Lutheran; his wife is Catholic.)

***Paul and Jeanne Simon**, who are both writing books for Continuum on the 1988 presidential race*

Simon is glad to be returning to his first calling. "The year I was out campaigning, I not only didn't get to do much writing, I didn't do much reading either. A candidate is expected to speak a great deal, and to write, read and reflect too little," he said, adding that he would never want to run for the presidency again. "I said when I withdrew from the campaign that running for president is like taking an ice cold shower: it's a great one-time experience but I'm not eager to repeat it."

Continuum plans a 30,000 first printing, and a marketing campaign that includes an author tour. An excerpt from the book in progress will appear in a July issue of the *New York Times Magazine*.

Jeanne Simon is a lawyer and a former politico as well; the Simons met when they were both state representatives in Illinois. She decided to write her book, she says, "when I looked around and realized there's never been a book about the life of the candidate's wife on the road. Rosalynn Carter talks about it in *First Lady from Plains* but that's only one part of it."

When the senator threw his hat into the ring in April 1987, Mrs. Simon says she realized that "this doesn't happen to someone every day" and began to keep a daily journal of her life from that point on until her husband's withdrawal from the race in April 1988.

She thought she knew what she was getting into when Simon declared his candidacy, Mrs. Simon says, having withstood her husband's successful Illinois senatorial bid. But she found out quickly that a presidential race is entirely different: "It's a lot more intense. Everything I said was scrutinized by the press so I had to be very careful. And the scheduling just never let up from day one. We hit the ground running," she explained.

In talking about her life on the road, Mrs. Simon added, "I saw things differently as a candidate's wife. Most of the time I was on my own as a surrogate for Paul but not getting the same treatment or reactions Paul would get. Ninety-nine percent of the time it was a really great trip, but the day I woke up and realized I had drycleaning in three states, I thought, 'there has to be a better way to do this.'"

The highlight of the year, Jeanne Simon found, was when the couple found out that the *Des Moines Register* was endorsing Simon. The low point came when his ratings dropped within a week of Gary

32 PUBLISHERS WEEKLY / JULY 15, 1988

An early announcement of a forthcoming title

try's weekly magazine—saying that a certain book by a certain author dealing with a certain subject will be published by a certain publisher at a certain date. Most likely, this will be the first public announcement of the book, and publication of this release in *Publishers Weekly* could well stimulate bookstore and library interest. (It also might, coincidentally, cancel or speed up another publisher's plans to bring out a work on the same subject.)

Formally, publicity work can begin with the arrival of galleys. As a matter of routine, specially bound, easy-to-read sets of these proofs are sent to those magazines whose opinions booksellers and librarians will consider when buying books. These periodicals, whose reviews will be printed well before the book is published, can be most influential in launching a book. A good review in these sources not only serves to move books into the stores, but can also engender enthusiasm in the publishing house itself.

In addition, bound galleys are sent to those major newspapers and magazines which need a long time to prepare their reviews. Finally, a limited number of bound galleys are sent to influential people who might have a special interest in the book, among them noted figures who could supply laudatory quotations which can be used for advertising or for blurbs on the jacket of the book.

With the sending of bound galleys, the process of word of mouth begins. The next step begins with the arrival of finished books. Each house has a list of reviewers and literary editors of newspapers and magazines to whom books are sent for review. Usually, a catalog is sent to these people several weeks or months before publication. The catalog describes the books, and along with it the publicity department will enclose a checklist of all the titles to be published. The reviewer examines the catalog and marks on the checklist those books which might be reviewed. The checklist is returned to the publicity department, which keeps records of which books to send to which reviewers.

The general review list is usually not enough, however. Each book being an individual case, the publicity department makes use of lists of influential people who might, because of the nature of the book, be especially interested in the subject, as well as of experts in certain fields, friends and colleagues of the author who might be useful in promoting the book, and so on. The total number of free books distributed by the publicity department might be as few as fifty or as many as several hundred.

Along with the book itself, it is common to enclose a news release and a photograph. The release will briefly describe the book and its author; the photograph—to be used in a newspaper or magazine—will be of the author, the subject of the book (if appropriate), the book's jacket, or possibly of an illustration from the book.

Because of the huge number of books published each year and the strictly limited amount of review space available, merely sending out galleys or books and releases and photographs is not enough. Reviewers and editors are flooded with books, and have the difficult task of choosing which ones to review. They will have to pay attention to works by well-known authors, and they will want to review those titles of special interest to themselves, keeping in mind that their book review sections must be balanced with a mixture of fiction, poetry, biography, current affairs, history, and so on.

However, the reviewer or book editor can use help in selecting books for review, and this help can be provided by the publicity department. If it is at all possible, the publicity director should personally see the book editor, frankly and honestly discussing the list and pointing out the highlights. A competent publicity director knows that not every reviewer can review every book and knows, too, which books will most likely interest which reviewer. The publicity director's guidance can be invaluable. Sometimes the editor or the publisher will either write to or see a reviewer: this special effort, if not used too often, can be helpful in obtaining a review by demonstrating an extra degree of enthusiasm. The importance of this enthusiasm, whether it comes from the publicity department, the editor, or the publisher, cannot be stressed too highly. And it is surprising how many books are helped by word of mouth spread by members of a publishing house other than the one which has published the book.

Everything discussed so far is more or less routine work for

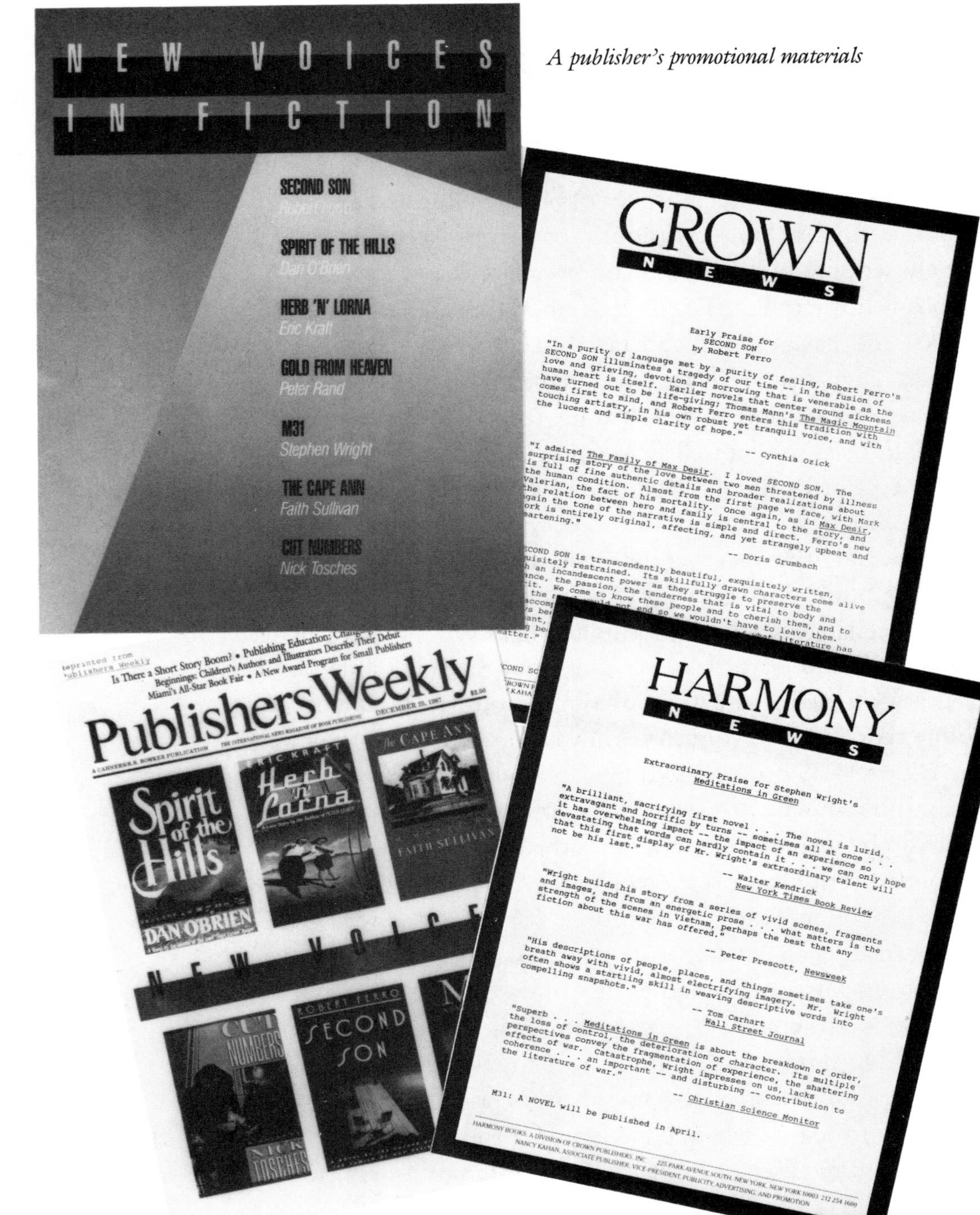

A publisher's promotional materials

a publicity department. It essentially consists of taking steps to see that books are reviewed or mentioned on the book pages of magazines and newspapers. Although there is no doubt that good reviews are of great importance, it is also true that poor reviews do not necessarily mean that a book will not sell. If the author has a sufficiently large following, if the timing and subject matter are right, and if the publisher does an unusually effective job of publicity and promotion, it is entirely possible for a book that receives a bad press to sell well or even become a best seller.

The above does not, incidentally, apply to children's books. Schools and libraries are the largest buyers of these titles, and their purchases are greatly influenced by reviews found in specialized magazines such as *School Library Journal, Kirkus Reviews,* the American Library Association's *Booklist, The Horn Book,* and the *Bulletin of the Center for Children's Books.* The larger school and public library systems have their own committees that select the books for purchase, thus in effect having their own reviewers whose advice is closely followed. The publicity and promotion departments of a publishing house that publishes children's books must of course keep in contact with these large local school and library systems and send them free review copies of each book as they do to the nationwide review media.

Beyond reviews for adult books, and considered even more effective, is work that will lead to bringing news of the book, or of the author, to those readers who are not necessarily influenced by book reviews. This off-the-book-page publicity generally calls for an author's willingness to participate personally in the promotion of a book. It also calls for careful, intelligent judgment on the part of the publicity director as to whether or not such treatment is feasible—it certainly

KIRKUS CHILDREN'S AND YOUNG-ADULT EDITION

President: Hope Kobak
Editor: Anne Larsen
Associate Editor: Jeffrey P. Zaleski
YA/Children's Editor: Joanna Rudge Long
Business Manager: Nancy Place
Editorial Assistant: Mary Daley

200 Park Avenue South, New York, N.Y. 10003 (212) 777-4554

Part II of Two Sections

January 15, 1988

Vol. LVI, No. 2

POINTERS (♦)

Books of unusually high quality.

- ♦ **Alderson, Sue Ann.** IDA AND THE WOOL SMUGGLERS. *Margaret K. McElderry/Macmillan.*
- ♦ **Fritz, Jean.** CHINA'S LONG MARCH. *Putnam.*
- ♦ **Hogrogian, Nonny.** THE CAT WHO LOVED TO SING. *Knopf.*
- ♦ **Lyon, George Ella.** BORROWED CHILDREN. *Orchard/Watts.*
- ♦ **Pullman, Philip.** SHADOW IN THE NORTH. *Knopf.*
- ♦ **Yorinks, Arthur.** COMPANY'S COMING. *Crown.*

Ahlberg, Allan
THE CLOTHES HORSE
and Other Stories
Illus. by Janet Ahlberg
Viking (32 pp.) $11.95
2/7 SBN: 670-81267-6

Six brief, whimsical stories with the air of extemporaneous bedtime tales told by a gifted parent, from the creators of *Each Peach Pear Plum*; each story is a logical (but zany) extension of a common phrase.

"The Clothes Horse" has been made by a magician, out of clothes; but even after all the clothes are appropriated, one by one, he retains a tenuous existence. "Life Savings" are bits of various ages stored up by a 70-year-old woman, resulting in curious behavior when she gets them out again. In "The Jack Pot," a beleaguered giant catches troublesome Jacks--till they form a football team and bother him more than ever. Then there are "No Man's Land," "The Night Train," and "God Knows"--God's answer to his own children when they ask him what else people invented (after spaceships and the Beatles) and what they did next. Janet Ahlberg's deft, carefully detailed illustrations add to the fun.

Cozy, comic, wry and wise, these rather British morsels may not be to the taste of every American child, but they're certainly worth a try. The avuncular voice suggets a read-aloud, but the stories' brevity will also make them attractive for independent reading. *(Fiction. 5–9)*

♦ **Alderson, Sue Ann**
IDA AND THE
WOOL SMUGGLERS
Illus. by Ann Blades
Margaret K. McElderry/
Macmillan (32 pp.)
$12.95
3/7 LC: 87-15487
SBN: 689-50440-3

Like the boy in Dalgliesh's *Bears on Hemlock Mountain*, Ida must traverse a bit of wild country, with a possible danger that does materialize, to do an important errand. She's taking bread to a family with a new baby, down the coast of her island off the west coast of Canada, when she hears smugglers whistling signals to one another. Bravely, she herds her favorite sheep and two new lambs to safety so that the smugglers don't get their fleece--and is rewarded with her dearest wish, being judged old enough to hold the baby.

The rather long text is clear and, with its linked themes of real danger and being old enough to take responsibility, maintains interest well. Blades' pastoral, watercolor

119 (C-11)

Important review publications for children's books

wouldn't be for most novels, for example—and whether or not the author possesses an attractive "public" personality. Writers write, and there is no reason to believe that a brilliant author will necessarily have the kind of personality that projects effectively in public appearances of any kind. Many authors are shy and are unable to help in publicizing their books. Others feel (mistakenly, because a purpose of writing a book is having it read by as many people as possible) that cooperating in the publicity for their book is somehow beneath them. For the most part, however, authors are more than willing—actually, most eager—to help in any way possible.

One medium for off-the-book-page publicity is the printed word—a newspaper or a magazine. If an author reveals timely, newsworthy, or even sensational information in a book, it may be worthy of a news or feature story or possibly an interview with the author, in a section of the newspaper or magazine other than the space reserved for books. A fashion editor might be interested in a book on fashion, just as a political editor would be interested in a book on politics, a food editor in a cookbook, or a financial editor in a book on the stock market. These interests could lead to articles that would be read even by those people (and there are far too many of them) who read only a few books a year.

There is little more that a publicity department can do with the printed word: through newspaper or magazine pieces a book can become a topic of conversation (controversy is helpful), or the author can become a "personality." These are, of course, highly effective means of publicizing a book, but there are other ways in which a publicity director will try to make a book known to the public. A few examples will suffice.

Star Tribune
MONDAY/November 14/1988 NEWSPAPER OF THE TWIN CITIES

'Indian Givers' finally get credit for their gifts

Staff Photo/Tom Sweeney

Anthropologist Jack Weatherford with a "goat-horned devil" mask from the Maya people of Guatemala and a "sun mask" from a tribe in Bolivia.

By George Monaghan/Staff Writer

When Jack McIver Weatherford first visited Kahl, the little German village where Europe's first nuclear plant was built, he assumed the facility's construction was the most significant event in the village's 2,000 year history.

He was wrong.

He hadn't heard about the potato. Hundreds of years earlier, someone planted a potato in the village. That crop, a gift from America's Indians, meant the difference between the community's continued existence and extinction.

In fact, the Macalester College anthropologist was to discover that the potato often meant the difference between life and death throughout much of the European continent and beyond.

The potato, Weatherford says, saved Ireland. Without it, Russia could never have become a superpower and Germany could never have started two world wars.

The influence of atomic energy paled in comparison. The potato "changed everything," says Weatherford. "It was a better staple. It protected them from periodic famine. It gave the people more calories per acre than grain and it didn't have to be milled. All they had to do was take it out of the ground and eat it. It gave them vitamin C. That reduced the virulence of their epidemics."

The Europeans owed all that and more to America's Indians. In South America, the Indians knew all about the uses of potatoes centuries before the European. Not only did European explorers bring back potatoes from the Indians, they brought maize, which they fed to their livestock and processed into oil.

Weatherford was fascinated. He wrote his Ph.D dissertation on what happened to the little German village, and then he went on to discover other facets of Indian life that made crucial differences in Europeans' lives, from their monetary systems to ways they governed themselves.

He began writing about it and his book on the subject, "Indian Givers," (Crown, $17.95) will be published next week.

Those who have seen the book say it's sure to provoke discussion about what Indians have given to whites and how whites have exploited them to get it.

"This is the kind of thing we should have been looking at years ago," said Zaida Giraldo, a medieval historian and an associate chancellor at the University of Massachusetts who did post doctoral work with Weatherford at Duke University. "I'm just surprised it's taken the historical

INDIANS Continued on page 5E

Two book reviews

The New York Times

Dinner Guests From Outer Space

COMPANY'S COMING
By Arthur Yorinks
Illustrated by David Small.
Unpaged. New York: Crown Publishers.
$11.95. (Ages 4 to 8)

By Alice Miller Bregman

I HAVE always admired people who, in the face of uninvited guests, are cool and calm. I'm one who flies into a tizzy at the mere thought of a dinner party. Last-minute drop-ins never bothered my mother, because my father was in the restaurant business and could bring home extras of whatever they were serving.

But I'm not sure my mother could ever have been as cool and unruffled as Shirley, the heroine of Arthur Yorinks's new story, "Company's Coming," on the day she's invited all her relatives to dinner and a flying saucer lands in her backyard. Certainly her husband, Moe, who has been "pleasantly tinkering in the yard," gets hysterical. More so, in fact, because Shirley doesn't.

I admire Shirley. "Moe, you had to buy *that* barbecue?" she chides him when she sees the flying saucer sitting next to the toolshed. "It's too big." Moe replies, "Shirl, it's not a barbecue." (The deadpan dialogue is irresistible, and at this point, readers and listeners tend to crack up.) Then two creatures from outer space, looking suspiciously like cockroaches wearing helmets, emerge from the oversized barbecue. " 'Greetings,' they spoke in English. 'We come in peace. Do you have a bathroom?' "

Now, if you think about that request, it doesn't make any sense — clearly these creatures have been

Illustration by David Small from "Company's Coming."

traveling for years on their way to another galaxy. What have they been doing all that time? Doesn't their spaceship have a bathroom? Yet it's absolutely logical. The first thing most children ask for whether they've been traveling for 10 minutes or 10 years is a bathroom. The genius of Arthur Yorinks's understated texts ("Louis the Fish," "Hey, Al") is that he knows what's truly important to youngsters.

The second thing children want is food, and that's just what Shirley, the consummate hostess, offers the travelers. "How about a sandwich, you must be hungry. . . . Would you like to stay for dinner?" The invitation is graciously accepted and the spacemen take off until 6 P.M., while Shirley and Moe rush inside to deal with this turn of events: Shirley goes straight to the kitchen, Moe rushes straight to the bedroom to phone the F.B.I., which in turn calls the Pentagon, which calls out the Army, the Air Force and the Marines. Moe is convinced that the creatures will vaporize not only their town, Bellmore, but the whole earth. The Pentagon seems worried as well. Not Shirley. Company's coming, and she has lots of work to do!

By 5:45 P.M., Shirley has organized the food and the relatives and changed into a long hostess gown. Moe, on the other hand, has managed to whip himself and some of the relatives into a panic. When the doorbell rings, Cousin Etta faints. No need to worry, however. The spacemen are very polite; they've even brought a hostess gift. Shirley is equally gracious, while Moe tries to rush them on their way and "Cousin Sheldon the loudmouth" tries to make conversation by asking about their trip.

"Well, we're on our way to check out a new planet," they say. "Our population has grown so quickly that we must branch out and find new places to live." This response only convinces me that the spacemen are cockroaches. Moe takes it much more seriously. "An invasion — we're doomed," he informs Cousin Harriet, while Shirley announces dinner. The visitors want her to open their gift first. "It'll knock you out," they tell her, and at that very moment, the soldiers and tanks armed with ballistic missiles invade. Amid the chaos, Shirley discovers that the gift is a blender. "And we don't even have one," she exclaims. "It was on sale!" the spacemen beam, and they all sit down to eat spaghetti and meatballs. Shirley has made extra!

This picture book is as satisfying as Shirley's meal. Arthur Yorinks's dialogue is as well timed as the best comedy act, and David Small has used pen and ink to outline his pale watercolors to capture the rhythm of the humor in, for example, the shrug of Shirley's shoulder, the twist of Moe's moustache or the way his hand fits in his pocket. You know these people. You've been to their house for dinner. So, if a spaceship could land in their backyard, what could happen at your house? □

Alice Miller Bregman, a former children's book editor, is a contributing editor and the children's book reviewer of Child magazine.

May 8, 1988

Although it is less common today than it was in the past, publishers sometimes give publication parties for their authors. These are often held in glamorous locations or unusual ones such as boats, railroad cars, or even exotic places that are relevant to the theme of the book. These parties can be costly, but they can serve to call attention to a given book, or even be occasions for the members of a publishing house to get to know members of the review media.

In addition, there are sometimes autographing parties given in bookstores, although these seem to be of little value, since most people don't really care for an autographed book unless the author is already famous. The appearance of an unknown author at a poorly attended autographing party could be most embarrassing for author and publisher alike. Some institutions, however, hold book fairs at which several authors appear, and these fairs can be useful: they may result in few copies sold at the time, but they help to spread the word of the book's publication. Some publishers, too, help to

LIFESTYLE

Billionaire Bashing

Writers are cashing in on nouvelle society

BY JENNET CONANT

Sex isn't nearly as fascinating as money in the 1980s. It used to be that summer brought forth a rash of steamy best sellers with page after breathless page of ardent prose. Alas, those days are gone. This year's beach books replace libido with intimate details of insider trading. The huge success of Tom Wolfe's "The Bonfire of the Vanities," a scathing satire of greed and decadence in New York society, has convinced publishers that Americans can't read enough about the vulgar rich. And why not? The raw material is just too good to ignore. Wall Street tycoon Ivan Boesky's downfall whet everyone's appetite for epic justice, and now hot behind him come the hotel czars Harry and Leona Helmsley on tax-fraud charges. Novelists, journalists, social critics and gossip columnists are lining up to dish the dirt on nouvelle society. "The drunkenness of wealth has passed and people are beginning to take a clinical look at the greed culture of the Reagan years," says Anthony Haden-Guest, ...

Who's who? *Dunne in his penthouse*

'Bucks, bucks, bucks': *Donald and Ivana Trump at the Metropolitan Club in New York, Saul and Gayfryd Steinberg attending the Metropolitan Costume Institute's 'Party of the Year'*

Telling tales: *Novelist Wolfe, social critic Lapham*

New money: *Kravis and Roehm, the spectacular Tisch-Steinberg megamerger*

86 NEWSWEEK MAY 30, 1988

NEWSWEEK MAY 30, 1988 87

An example of off-the-book page coverage

arrange lecture tours for an author, if the author is articulate and personable, and these too can greatly stimulate interest in a book.

The list of possibilities for publicity is almost endless, but of all means of creating interest in a book, the most effective in recent years has been the television appearance. Television, of course, reaches an enormous audience, many of whom are not regular book readers, but who will occasionally purchase a book if persuaded to do so. And television, as has been demonstrated, can be most persuasive. There are, unfortunately, very few programs devoted to books alone, but an appearance by an interesting author on one or many "talk" shows can result in the sale of many copies of the book.

However, as effective as television (and, to a lesser extent, radio) appearances are, a wise publicity director will know that the large majority of authors are not suitable for use on these media for a number of reasons. One reason is that most authors do not have the sense of showmanship necessary for television appearances. Next, unfortunately, television programs don't want most authors as guests. It is useless even to try to place an unknown author (a first novelist, for example, would not even be considered except in very rare cases) on a television program unless the book is of unusually wide interest and is, preferably, a controversial one. Even a well-known literary figure, unless he or she is especially colorful, will find it impossible to compete for television time with the author of a book who is best known in another field such as show business or sports, psychology or cooking.

Undoubtedly, television can do a great deal to influence the sales of a book—repeated appearances are best—but undoubtedly, too, it can be used by a very small number of authors in the promotion of their books.

TOP SEVENTY MARKETS AS OF JANUARY 1988

1.New York
2.Los Angeles
3.Chicago
4.Philidelphia
5.San Francisco/Oakland
6.Boston
7.Detroit
8.Dallas/Ft.Worth
9.Washington, D.C.
10.Houston
11.Cleveland/Akron
12.Atlanta
13.Tampa/St.Petersburg
14. Seattle/Tacoma
15.Minneapolis
16.Miami/Ft. Lauderdale

36.Raleigh/Durham
37.Oklahoma City
38.Grand Rapids/Kalamazaa
39.Buffalo
40.Birmingham/Anniston
41.Memphisam/Anniston
42.Salt Lake City
43.San Antonio
44.Providence/New Bedford
45.Norfolk/Portsmouth/Newport
46.Harrisburg/Lancaster/Lebanon/York
47.Wilkes Barre/Scranton
48.Louisville
49.Dayton
50.Greenboro/Winston-Salem
51.Charleston/Huntingiton,WV
bany/Schenectedy/Troy
sa
t Palm Beach/Ft.Pierce
hmond/Petersburg/
rlottesville
eveport
tle Rock/Pine Bluff
nt/Saginaw/Bay City
xsonville
ile/Pensicola
hita/Hutchinson
sno/Visalia
xville
edo
uquerque
en Bay/Appleton
acuse

JUDITH KRANTZ TILL WE MEET AGAIN

Barbara Marks Ext.782

Satellite Publicity Tour: How it Works

Satellite publicity tours have become valuable additions
to our publicity campaigns. During th
we have completed successful tours wit
Desmond Morris, Chuck Berry, and Billy

Satellite tours enable an author to ap
television in local markets without se
the road. The author spends several h
or Los Angeles studio and is interview
of morning, noon, and evening talk and
target markets according to media rati
attached list) and the audience approp

Satellite tours are becoming increasin
television hosts, who realize they hav
to book a celebrity guest who otherwis
to their city. Production companies a
booking top shows in top markets.

Judy Krantz will travel via satellite
two days on Tuesday, September 13 and
September 14.

CROWN PUBLISHERS, INC., 225 PARK AVENUE SOUTH, NEW

You Are Invited
To Meet

Steven Kellogg
at
The White Rabbit

Monday, November 30, 1987

Mr. Kellogg will present a special storytelling at 3:00 p.m., followed by autographing until 5:00 p.m.

The following titles will be available, and may be purchased in advance:

"A" My Name is Alice (11.95, hardcover; 3.95, paperback)
New! *Aster Aadvark's Alphabet Adventure (13.00)*
Best Friends (12.95)
The Boy Who Was Followed Home (11.95, hardcover; 3.95, paper)
Can I Keep Him? (12.95, hardcover; 3.95, paperback)
Chicken Little (13.00, hardcover; 3.95, paperback)
The Day Jimmy's Boa Ate the Wash (10.95, hardcover; 3.95, paper)
How Much is a Million? (15.00, hardcover; 2.95, paperback)
Island of the Skog (12.95, hardcover; 3.95, paperback)
Jimmy's Boa Bounces Back (11.95, hardcover; 3.95, paperback)
Leo, Zack and Emmie Together Again (8.95)
Much Bigger Than Martin (3.95, paperback)
The Mysterious Tadpole (11.95, hardcover; 3.95, paperback)
The Mystery of the Flying Pumpkin (3.50, paperback)
The Mystery of the Missing Red Mitten (2.95, paperback)
The Mystery of the Stolen Blue Paint (3.50, paperback)
Paul Bunyan (15.00, hardcover; 4.95, paperback)
Pecos Bill (13.00)
Pinkerton Behave (11.95, hardcover; 3.95, paperback)
New! *Prehistoric Pinkerton (12.95)*
Ralph's Secret Weapon (3.95, paperback)
A Rose For Pinkerton (12.95, hardcover; 3.95, paperback)
Tallyho Pinkerton (10.95, hardcover; 3.95, paperback)
Won't Somebody Play With Me (9.95, hardcover; 3.95, paperback)

Publicity, on a satellite tour and in the bookstore

Effective as well is a tour for the author to a few or several cities throughout the country, making use of each stop for local newspaper interviews, television and radio appearances, and meetings with local reviewers and booksellers. However, just as in the case of television programs, these tours must be limited to special authors, since once again there would be little interest in appearances by or interviews with relatively unknown authors. In addition, the costs of such tours can be high in both time and money since the author is normally accompanied by a member of the publicity department or, in some cases, a local representative—either the publisher's sales representative or someone hired especially for the job.

Satellite publicity tours have become valuable additions to publicity campaigns for big-name authors. The author stays in a New York or Los Angeles studio and is interviewed via satellite by hosts of local television talk shows. This allows the author to do many more interviews and is far less expensive.

The most costly way of promoting a book—by advertising it—has been left for last, since many publishers believe it is far less effective than do their authors. In fact, many publishers say that they advertise more to please their authors than to sell books.

Initial advertising in trade journals such as *Publishers Weekly* or *Library Journal* is considered worthwhile as a form of announcement to the librarian and bookseller. This advertising also demonstrates confidence in a book. Beyond that, advertising in magazines and newspapers and on radio and television, though more prevalent than in the past, is very costly, and the budget for most books does not leave room for much or any of it. Curiously, it is widely believed that advertising is usefully employed only *after* a book has started to sell (it can turn a good seller into a best seller), and as a

Black Sand

by *William J. Caunitz*

In 1984 Crown published *One Police Plaza* by William Caunitz, then an unknown New York City policeman. Caunitz followed with *Suspects* in 1986. Both books have become international best sellers and both have sold more than 2.5 million copies.

Caunitz's sensational new novel begins with a massacre in a Greek seaside resort, an atrocity that sets off a deadly struggle to find a stolen ancient artifact. The search leads two policemen—Det. Lt. Teddy Lucas of the New York Police Department and Maj. Andreas Vassos of the Hellenic National Police—through their own underworlds and into the vicious games played by multimillionaire collectors. Assisting them are a KGB officer responsible for liaison with the NYPD, a stunningly beautiful expert on ancient manuscripts, and a wonderfully mixed bag of New York cops. *Black Sand* is a compelling, high-speed narrative that will capture readers from the very first page. 448 pages. **• 150,000-copy first printing and $100,000 national launch budget • National author tour • Promotional galley •** March. (571323) $17.95. 12-copy display unit (572265) $215.40

© Jerry Bauer

CROWN PUBLISHERS, INC.

A Casual Brutality

by *Neil Bissoondath*

Anne Marcoux

"A writer already almost awesomely mature." (*Financial Times*) "He has engaged his art to the dangerous forces that sway the world." (*Washington Post*) "I'm staggered by the talent." V.S. Naipaul (About Bissoondath's collection of short stories, *Digging Up the Mountains*)

Naipaul's nephew has written a novel of tremendous power and linguistic grace about a man's personal dilemma in the face of political disintegration. Raj Ramsingh, a doctor who returns to his birthplace of Casa quemade; his psychological dislocation in the face of increasing violence and the inevitable tragedy that results. A book that asks: is it possible for a good man to live a good life in a place going bad. A rich, compelling narrative, almost mezmerizing in its intensity. **• 30,000-copy first printing and $30,000 national launch budget • Author tour • Call 212-254-1600, X 775 for an advance galley! • Promotional postcards • New Voices in Fiction •**

CLARKSON N. POTTER, INC.
A MEMBER OF THE CROWN PUBLISHING GROUP

Publishers Weekly is published weekly by Bowker Magazine Group, Cahners Magazine Division, Terrence M. McDermott, President; Carroll V. Dowden, Group Vice President; Jerry D. Neth, Vice President/Publishing Operations; J. J. Walsh, Financial Vice President/Magazine Division; Thomas J. Dellamaria, Vice President/Production & Manufacturing. Bowker Magazine Group is also an affiliate of R. R. Bowker Co., Gordon Graham, Chairman of the Board; Ira Siegel, President. Copyright © 1988 by Reed Publishing, USA; Saul Goldweitz, Chairman; Ronald G. Segel, President & Chief Executive Officer; Robert L. Krakoff, Executive Vice President; William M. Platt, Sr. Vice-President. Printed in the U.S.A. SUBSCRIPTION: U.S.A.: 1 year $94, 2 years $160, 3 years $225. Canada: 1 year $177, 2 years $300, 3 years $420. Air delivery to all other countries: 1 year $250, 2 years $425, 3 years $595. (Remit in U.S. funds only.) Single copy $5.00, announcements $10.00 each. Prepayment required. Send single copy requests to: Publishers Weekly, P. O. Box 1979, Marion, OH 43302. PUBLICATION ADDRESS: Publishers Weekly, P.O. Box 1979, Marion, OH 43302. *Address editorial and advertising correspondence to* 249 West 17th Street, New York, NY 10011; telephone: 212/645-0067; telex: 12-7703. *Address circulation correspondence and changes of address to* Publishers Weekly, P.O. Box 1979, Marion, OH 43302; telephone 1-800-669-1002; in Alaska, Hawaii, Canada, and all other countries, telephone: 614-382-3322. Second-class postage paid at New York, N.Y., and additional mailing offices. **POSTMASTER:** Send address changes to *Publishers Weekly*, P.O. Box 1979, Marion, OH 43302. Cahners Publishing Company, a Division of Reed Publishing USA ☐ Specialized Business Magazines for Building & Construction, Manufacturing, Foodservice & Lodging, Electronics & Computers, Interior Design, Printing, Publishing, Industrial Research & Technology, Health Care, and Entertainment. ☐ Specialized Consumer Magazines: *American Baby* and *Modern Bride*.

CROWN PUB

THE RAFFI CHRISTMAS TREASURY: 14 Illustrated Songs and Musical Arrangements
Illustrated by Nadine Bernard Westcott.
A sumptuous, joyfully illustrated collection of all the traditional carols and original songs on *Raffi's Christmas Album*—including musical arrangements for all! (Watch Raffi in concert this fall on The Disney Channel.) September. All ages. (568063) $17.95

THOMAS THE TORTOISE
Written and illustrated by Graham Jeffery.
The sensitive story of a tortoise whose friends help him overcome his shortcomings. September. Ages 3–6. (570432) $9.95

RABBITS ON ROLLER SKATES!
By Jan Wahl.
Illustrated by David Allender.
First published in 1986 as part of the *It's Great to Read*™ series, those zany rabbits are on the loose again in a new hardcover, jacketed edition. August. Ages 3–6. (569973) $6.95

DOLLARS AND CENTS FOR HARRIET: A Money Concept Book.
By Betsy and Giulio Maestro.
The ever-popular Harriet helps young readers learn how coins make up a dollar and how dollars add up as well. September. Ages 3–6. (569582) $12.95

THE HIDDEN LIFE SERIES
Photographed in color by Dwight Kuhn.
Text by David M. Schwartz.
The "what", "how" and "why of nature, revealed in three exciting, closeup nature walks. October. Ages 5 up. $12.95 each
THE HIDDEN LIFE OF THE POND (570602)
THE HIDDEN LIFE OF THE FOREST (570580)
THE HIDDEN LIFE OF THE MEADOW (570599)

TV sup... bestsell... explair... he can. ... game to ... terbacks ... her ... Amer... w...

cub-l... ava... Septe...

LITTLE TREE
by e. e. cummings.
Illustrated by Deborah Kogan Ray.
cumming's magical Christmas poem in picture-book form. "Small listeners will smile with sympathy and satisfaction." —*School Library Journal* (starred). Ages 5–9. (565986) $9.95
10-copy prepack (570823) $99.50

consequence very little money is budgeted for the advertising of all but a limited number of what seem to be mass-appeal books. Although a book will probably be advertised if there are early indications of extra monies that the book will earn—such as a good paperback sale or a movie sale—the fact is that little money is spent on advertising most books before they are proven sellers.

Advertising is one way of persuading people to buy a book, but as we have seen, it is expensive. Fortunately there are other ways available which can be even more effective. The essential element in finding these ways of letting the public know of a book's availability and interest is an imaginative publicity department, whose job in its way can be as creative as that of any other individual or group taking part in the long and complicated process of publishing a book.

DESKTOP PUBLISHING

Over the past decade there have been significant changes in the technology of book publishing. A number of these changes, which have affected all those involved in the creation and production of books, have been noted throughout this book. Others have seemed too complex for inclusion in an introductory volume of this kind. One change, however, is worthy of special mention: the emergence and development of what is known as desktop publishing.

Desktop publishing, as its name suggests, allows a publishing house to be established on the top of a desk. It represents an enormous saving of both time and money. With the use of a personal computer system and the appropriate software, it is now possible to edit, design, illustrate, lay out, and typeset a book in a relatively short time and without a large staff and a staggering budget.

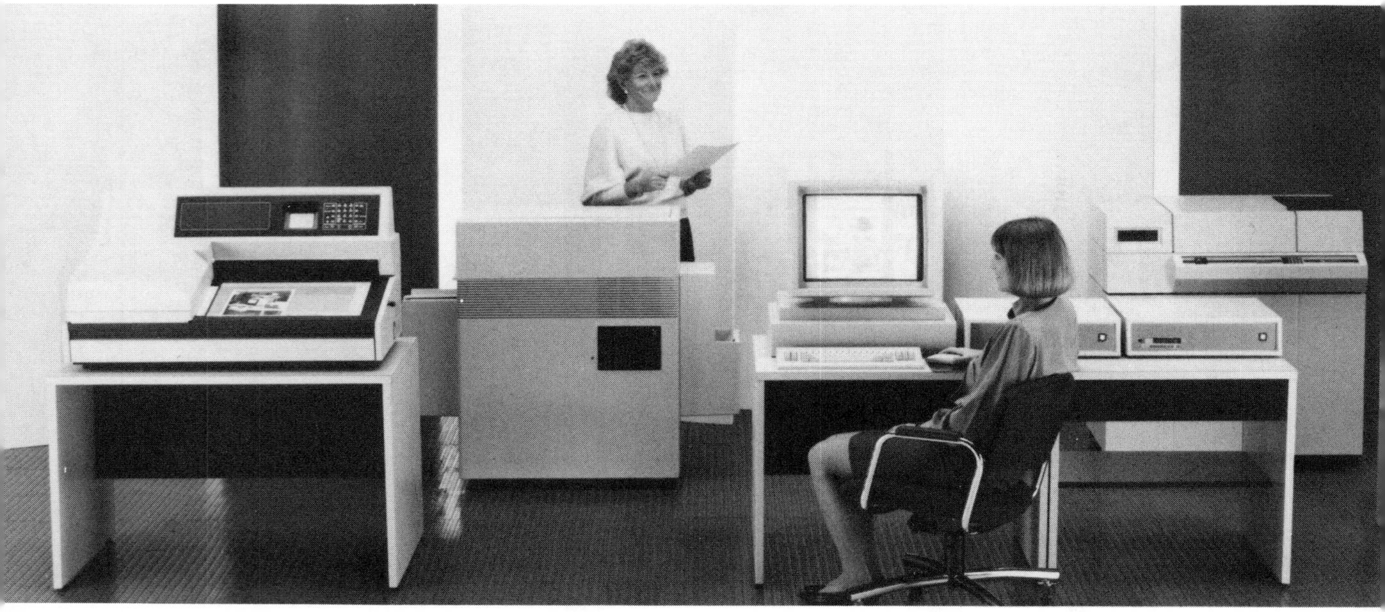

The Compugraphic Automated Publishing System (CAPS™)
Left to right: *graphic scanner, plain-paper printer, main computer with keyboard and screen, laser imagesetter*

Compugraphic graphic scanner

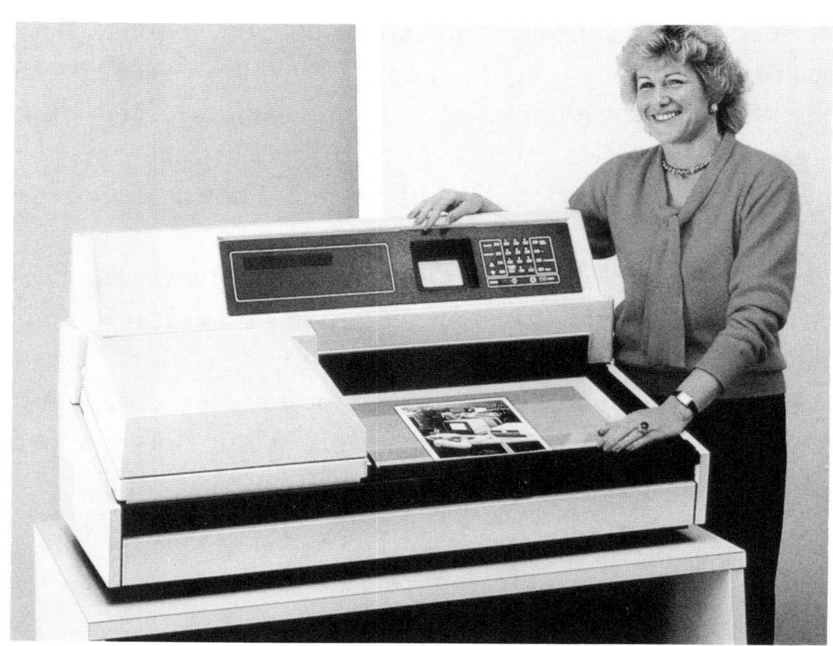

The Compugraphic Automatic Publishing System(CAPS™) (facing page) *is an example of a state-of-the-art desktop publishing system. Text can be written at the keyboard or prekeyboarded at a different computer or word processor. Editing and design occur at the keyboard. The screen shows the designer the actual typeface in the correct size. Any text changes or movement of elements is shown on the screen. Pages are made automatically from instructions given by the designer. Line art can be "drawn" on the computer using programs like Apple's MacDraw or optically scanned on the graphic scanner. The plain-paper copier prints low-cost, nonreproduction quality proofs. The laser imagesetter gives high-quality proofs. This system allows the publisher to go from written word to the printer at one location.*

Apple's Macintosh and LaserWriter™ is a less sophisticated and less expensive desktop publishing system.

Desktop publishing eliminates the need for outside typesetters and artists. With the use of a relatively inexpensive computer, type can be set in the office. The results can be checked at once and corrections made easily and at no extra cost. Full page makeup, too, can be done on the computer. Changes can be made on the screen, and there is no need for galleys, or for cutting and pasting.

With the use of painting and drawing programs, digitizers, image scanners, and other graphic tools, it is possible for artists to create images on the screen; this artwork, combined on the same page with the text, can be examined on the screen before printing. Once again, by this method, correction is simplified.

Finally, type and art, in page format, can be output in the office, by means of a laser printer, which looks much like an office photocopier and uses regular paper. The results are already surprisingly good, and in time they may equal typeset quality. These pages can then go to the offset printer.

Desktop publishing will enable a writer's words and ideas to reach a large number of readers more economically and efficiently than ever before. It represents progress, and as such it is welcome, but it is important to remember the ultimate reason for desktop publishing and all the other tools and procedures described in this volume—the books themselves, and the enrichment and pleasure they bring to the reader.

As we have seen, books don't just happen: a great amount of talent, skill, and hard work is involved each step of the way. There are techniques and methods and changing technologies, yet no book could exist without the miracle that lies behind it—the human mind.

GLOSSARY

AA (author's alteration) A correction made in galleys by the author.

acetate A sheet of clear plastic film taped over artwork as an overlay.

acknowledgment Part of a book, generally in the front matter, acknowledging thanks or credit to those who helped with the book.

ad card Part of a book, generally in the front matter, listing other books by the same author, also called card page.

advance Payment by the publisher to the author before the book is published, to be deducted from future earnings.

appendix Additional useful information related to but not part of the main text of a book, generally found in the back matter.

artwork The assembled parts of a mechanical to be used as camera copy.

ascender That part of a lower-case letter which extends above the main body of that letter, as in *d* or *b*.

back matter All material that follows the main body of the text, such as appendix, bibliography, glossary, index.

bibliography A list of source materials and supplementary reading relevant to the book, usually a part of the back matter.

binding die An engraving used to impress letters or a design on the binding of a hardbound book.

bleed An illustration which extends to the very edge of the trimmed page, the part of the printed page that will be trimmed off.

blues (blueprints) Photoprints made from the assembled films used in making offset plates. Blues serve as final proofs.

blurb A description of the book printed on the flaps or the back of the jacket.

boldface A type used for emphasis, thicker than the text type with which it is used.

BOM proofs Proofs, especially cut and bound for easier reading, which are submitted to book clubs or reviewers, or are used for publicity purposes.

bulk The thickness of paper, or sometimes the thickness of a book.

calender To pass paper between cylinders under pressure. The way in which this is done determines the smoothness and glossiness of the surface of the paper.

camera copy Material to be photographed for platemaking.

camera-separated artwork Artwork which is to be separated into different colors for printing by use of a camera.

caption Identification of an illustration, usually printed under that illustration.

case In printing, a compartmented tray in which type is kept; in binding, the covers of a hardbound book.

casting The procedure in which molten metal is forced against a mold, then cooled and hardened to produce type or lines of type.

castoff An estimate of the number of pages a book will be when it is set in type.

chapter opening The first page of a chapter.

chapter title The title of a chapter.

character Each letter, numeral, symbol, and punctuation mark of a font.

character count The number of letters, symbols, numerals, punctuation marks, and spaces that a manuscript contains.

cold type Type set by direct impression without the use of metal.

color separation The process of separating full color into the primary printing colors by means of photography with color filters.

color swatches Specimens or samples which indicate the precise color to be used in printing.

contents A list of the entire contents of a book, generally part of the front matter.

copy Any material to be composed or photographed for printing.

copyright The exclusive right, given by law for a number of years, to make and sell a work of literature, music, or art. In the case of a book (which cannot be copyrighted unless printed and sold), a notice to this effect must be printed either on the title page or on the reverse of the title page.

crop To select a part of an image, eliminating the areas around it.

CRT Cathode ray tube, a video display.

dedication An inscription, generally part of the front matter, dedicating a book to a person, persons, or a cause.

descender That part of a lower-case letter which extends below the main body of that letter, as in *p* or *y*.

digitized type Type stored as digital dot or stroke patterns.

disk (disc) A flat piece of plastic coated with a magnetic substance. A computer stores data on this coating. Also called a magnetic disk.

display type Letters set larger than the text, to draw attention.

double-spread Two facing pages, designed as a single unit.

dummy Pages which show the size, shape, and general appearance of a book, often including a rough layout with the position of text and illustrations.

EA (editorial alteration) A correction made in galleys by the editor or designer.

endpapers Folded paper, sturdier than that used for the text and often colored or decorated, pasted to the insides of the front and back covers of a book for binding.

estimate A calculation of the cost of a book made before production begins.

extract Special text matter set off typographically or by the use of indentation from the main body of the text.

f & g's Printed sheets, folded and gathered in proper sequence, preliminary to binding.

flat Assemblage of films, stripped on goldenrod paper in their proper arrangement, for use in making offset plates.

flat sheets Printed sheets before they have been folded for binding.

flush A line of type, set to line up at right or left.

folio A page number.

font The complete assortment of type, of one face and size.

footnote Supplementary notation at the bottom of a page which refers to material on that page.

foreword An introductory statement, usually by someone other than the author. Part of the front matter.

fountain, ink The device in a printing press which stores ink and then supplies it to rollers.

four-color presses Printing presses that can apply four different colors simultaneously.

frontispiece An illustration facing the title page of a book.

front matter All material which precedes the main text of a book.

full measure The full width of a line of type, flush with both margins.

galley A shallow metal drawer or tray in which type and cuts are kept after setting

galley proofs (galleys) The first proofs pulled, before the type has been divided into pages.

gathering Bringing together the signatures of a book for binding.

glossary A list of special terms used in a book, with their definitions.

goldenrod A specially treated orange yellow paper, on which films are positioned for the making of offset plates.

gravure An intaglio method of printing; the printing areas which retain the ink on the plate are depressed.

half title The title of the book set in smaller letters than on the title page and usually found on the first page of the book.

hot type Type set by cast metal by hand or by machine.

imposition The arrangement of pages in a press form, so that they will be in proper sequence for binding when folded.

impression cylinder The cylinder that presses the pages against the inked surfaces for printing.

indentation The setting of a line of type to less than the full width of the page.

index A list of proper nouns, terms, and sometimes concepts used in the text, with their corresponding page numbers, which is part of the back matter of a book.

inside margin (gutter) The distance from the inner edge of the page to the beginning of the type area.

Intertype A typesetting machine which casts each line as a solid line of type; it is similar to Linotype.

introduction A formal statement of the scope and purpose of the book, sometimes part of the front matter and sometimes part of the text itself.

italics Slanted letters, used in the text for emphasis.

justify To space out lines to the correct uniform width.

key plate In color printing, the plate (usually black) containing the outline which is used as a guide for the other colors.

layout The drawing or sketch of all the elements on a page in proper position.

leading The space between lines of type.

line art Copy that contains only solid blacks and whites and thus can be reproduced without gradation in tone.

Linotype A typesetting machine which casts each line as a solid line of metal type.

lower case Uncapitalized letters of the alphabet.

makeup Arrangement of all elements—type and illustration—into page form.

margin The white space on all four sides of the printed area of a page.

mechanical Camera-ready pasteup of all elements on one piece of artboard for use in offset platemaking.

negative A transparent photographic film on which light values and images are reversed (the black shows as white, left is right, etc.).

offset (blanket) cylinder A cylinder onto which a rubber blanket is attached and which transfers the image from the plate to the paper in offset printing.

opaquing Painting out on a negative the areas that are not wanted on a plate.

page proofs (pages) Copy of the type after division into page form.

part title The title or number of a major part of a book, generally printed on a separate page preceding that part.

PE (printer's error) An error made by the compositor.

perfect binding A method of binding, without stitching or sewing, in which the signatures are held together by an adhesive.

photostats An economically reproduced photograph made with the use of special equipment, often used for layouts and dummies.

pica A measurement, which equals twelve points or approximately one-sixth of an inch, used by printers to measure lines.

plant cost Nonrecurring expenses in the manufacture of a book, such as composition and plates.

point The basic unit of type measurement; there are approximately 72 points to an inch.

positive A print made from a negative, showing the original light values and images.

progressive proofs (progs) Proofs used in color process printing which show each color alone and then in combination with other colors.

proofs Trial impressions of composed type or illustrations, taken to correct errors and make changes.

registering Precisely superimposing in correct relationship the various colors in color printing.

register marks Crosses or other devices used as a guide to registering.

repros (reproduction proofs) Proofs on specially coated paper to be used as camera copy for offset platemaking.

roman The ordinary upright type style, as opposed to slanted italics.

rough layout A preliminary sketch of a layout meant for general effect and not detail.

royalty The author's percentage of the proceeds from the sales of a book, generally based on the retail price.

running heads The book, part, or chapter title repeated at the top of each page of a book.

scanner An optical device that is able to scan images such as photographs or drawings and record the information digitally.

serif A short line extending from the main stroke of a letter in some typefaces.

signature A folded, printed sheet of a book, usually sixteen or thirty-two pages.

sinkage The distance from the top of the page to the highest element on a type page.

small caps Capital letters that are smaller in size than regular capitals.

Smyth sewing A method of binding by means of threads which are passed through each signature and locked at the back.

specifications, type The complete instructions for composition.

spine The part of the binding that connects the two covers.

staining Coloring the edges of a book.

text type The type used for the main body of the text as opposed to the headings.

title page The part of the front matter that contains the title of the book, the name of the author, and the name of the publisher.

trim size The size of the pages after the paper has been trimmed.

typeface Any design of type, including the full range of characters (letters, numbers, and punctuation marks) in every size.

typescript Typewritten copy.

type size The size of type designated in points.

upper case Capital letters.

value The degree of lightness or darkness of a tone or color.

BIBLIOGRAPHY

American Booksellers Association. *A Manual on Bookselling.* Eds. Robert Hale, Allan Marshall, and Ginger Curwen. 4th ed. New York: Harmony Books, 1987.

Bailey, Herbert S., Jr. *The Art and Science of Book Publishing.* Austin: University of Texas Press, 1970.

Bove, Tony, Cheryl Rhodes, and Wes Thomas. *The Art of Desktop Publishing.* New York: Bantam Books, 1987.

Chappell, Warren. *A Short History of the Printed Word.* New York: Alfred A. Knopf, 1970.

Gates, Frieda. *How to Write, Illustrate, and Design Children's Books.* Monsey, N.Y.: Lloyd-Simone Publishing Company, 1986.

Hands, Nancy S. *Illustrating Children's Books.* New York: Prentice Hall Press, 1986.

Holt, Robert Lawrence. *How to Publish, Promote, and Sell Your Own Books.* New York: St. Martin's Press, 1985.

International Paper Company. *Pocket Pal.* 13th ed. New York, 1983.

Lee, Marshall. *Bookmaking.* New York: R. R. Bowker, 1979.

Makuta, Daniel J., and William F. Lawrence. *The Complete Desktop Publisher.* Greensboro, N.C.: COMPUTE! Publications, 1986.

Shulevitz, Uri. *Writing with Pictures: How to Write and Illustrate Children's Books*. New York: Watson-Guptill Publications, 1985.

University of Chicago. *The Chicago Guide to Preparing Electronic Manuscripts*. Chicago: University of Chicago Press, 1987.

——. *The Chicago Manual of Style*. 13th ed. Chicago: University of Chicago Press, 1982.

Wilson, Adrian. *The Design of Books*. New York: Reinhold Publishing Corporation, 1967.

INDEX